11+
Non-verbal Reasoning

TESTBOOK 2

Standard & Multiple-choice 30 Minute Tests

Dr Stephen C Curran

Edited by Autumn McMahon

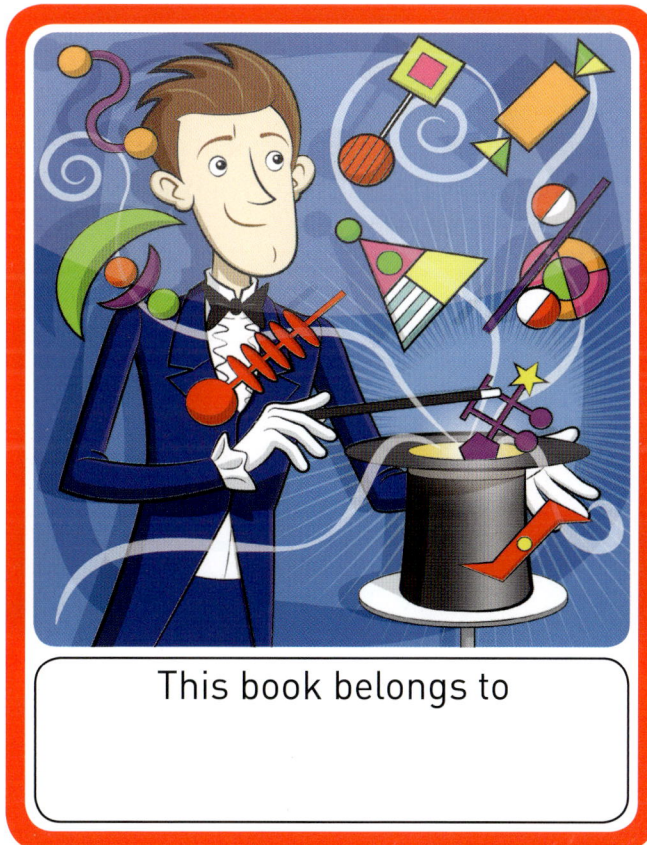

ae
PUBLICATIONS

Accelerated Education Publications Ltd

Guidance notes for parents

These practice papers can be completed as standard or multiple-choice tests.

Multiple-choice Tests

Answers are entered onto the answer sheets at the back of the book. The actual test would be marked by a computer but, for the purposes of these practice tests, you will need to mark it yourself. It is important for your child to treat it like the real thing and record an answer in the appropriate box by drawing a clear line through their chosen box with a pencil. Mistakes should be carefully rubbed out and not crossed out since in the actual test this would not be correctly recorded by the computer.

Standard Tests

Ask your child to circle the answers as instructed in each section. Mistakes should be crossed through with a single line and the correct answer written clearly.

Marking and Feedback

The answers are provided at the back of this book. Only these answers are allowed. One mark should be given for each correct answer. Do not deduct marks for wrong answers. Do not allow half marks or 'the benefit of the doubt', as this might mask a child's need for extra help in the topic and does not replicate the real exam conditions. Always try to be positive and encouraging. Talk through any mistakes with your child and work out together how to arrive at the right answer.

Timing

This testbook contains 8 practice papers. Each paper should take about 30 minutes, however it is more important that a child completes the paper accurately and does not rush their answers. Children will speed up naturally with practice.

Non-verbal Reasoning Test 1
Section A

To the left of each of the lines below there are five squares arranged in order. One of these squares has been left empty. Find which one of the five squares on the right should take the place of the empty square.

Example

a   **b**   c   d   e

Now do the questions below. Circle the correct answer.

1)

a   b   c   d   e

2)

a   b   c   d   e

3)

a   b   c   d   e

4)

a   b   c   d   e

5)

6)

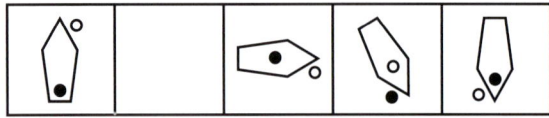 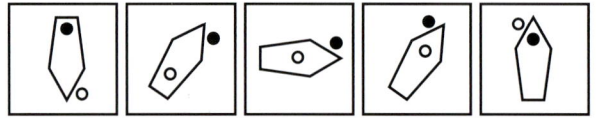

7)

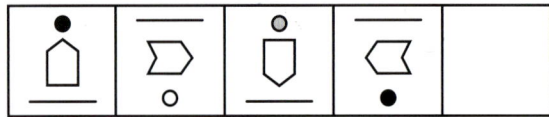 

8)

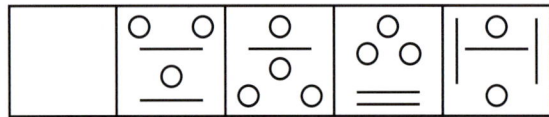 

9)

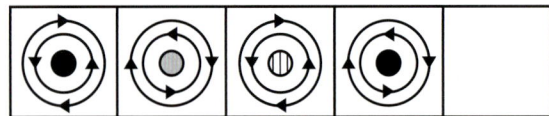 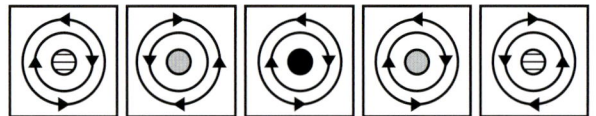

Score

Section B

In the big square on the left of each line below, one of the small squares has been left empty. One of the five figures on the right should fill the empty square. Find this figure.

Example

Now do the questions below. Circle the correct answer.

1)

2)

3)

4)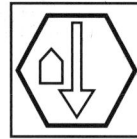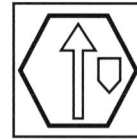

     a   **b**   **c**   **d**   **(e)**

5)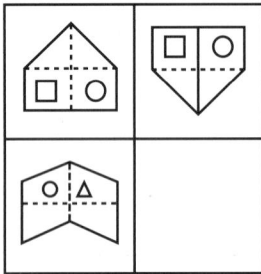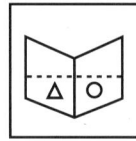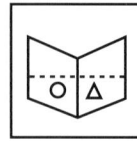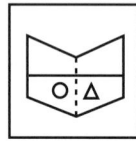

     a   **b**   **(c)**   **d**   **e**

6)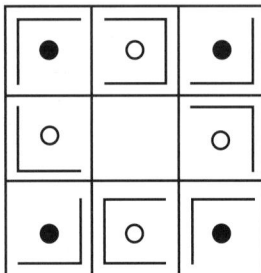

     a   **b**   **(c)**   **d**   **e**

7)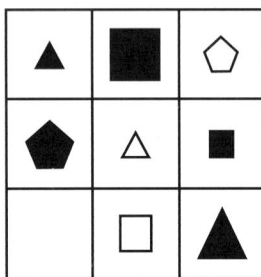

     a   **(b)**   **c**   **d**   **e**

8)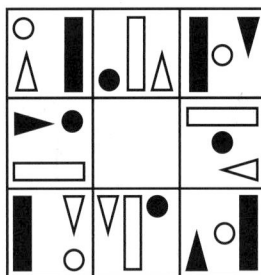

     a   **b**   **c**   **(d)**   **e**

Score 7/4

Section C

In each of the rows below there are five figures. Find one figure in each row that is **most unlike** the other four.

Example

   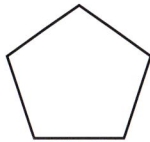   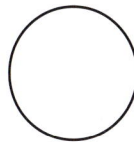   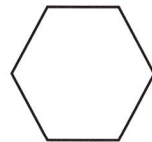

a   **b**   **c**   **d**   **e**

Now do the questions below. Circle the correct answer.

1)

a   **b**   **c**   **d**   **e**

2)

a   **b**   **c**   **d**   **e**

3)

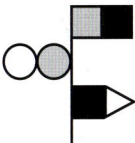   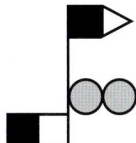   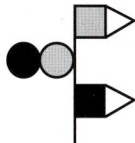   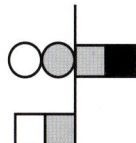   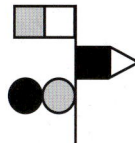

a   **b**   **c**   **d**   **e**

4)

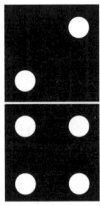 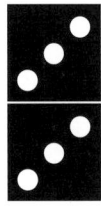 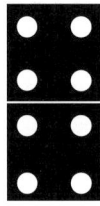 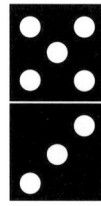 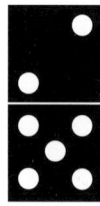

a   **b**   **c**   **d**   **e**

5)

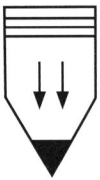  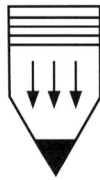  

a   **b**   **c**   **d**   **e**

6)

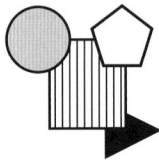 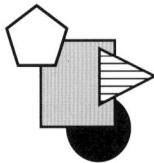  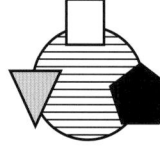 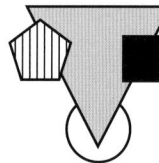

a   **b**   **c**   **d**   **e**

7)

 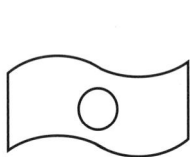   

a   **b**   **c**   **d**   **e**

8)

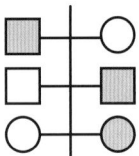 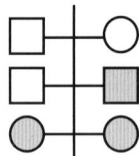 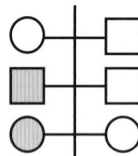 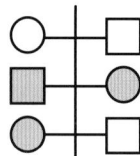 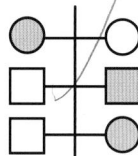

a   **b**   **c**   **d**   **e**

Score

Section D

The following figures correspond to the codes next to them. You must decide how the code letters go with the figures and then find the correct code for the Test Figure.

Example

TEST FIGURE

↑	O
	V

⬇	N
	W

←	M
	V

↑	?	O	N	M	O	M
	?	V	V	W	W	V
		a	b	c	(d)	e

Now do the questions below. Circle the correct answer.

1)

♡♡♡	C
	W

♡♡♡	D
	X

♡♡♡	D
	Y

TEST FIGURE

♡♡♡	?	D	C	C	D	D
	?	X	Y	W	W	Y
		(a)	b	c	d	e

2)

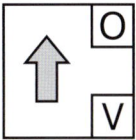 K / F

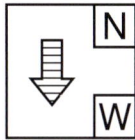 M / G

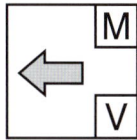 L / F

TEST FIGURE

⊕	?	L	M	M	K	K
	?	G	G	F	F	G
		a	b	c	(d)	e

3)

▲	C
	W

◇	D
	Z

◆	C
	X

TEST FIGURE

▽	?	D	C	D	C	D
	?	Z	X	W	Z	X
		(a)	b	c	d	e

4)

△△△	F
	O

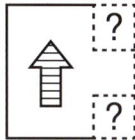 E / R

○○	F
	P

TEST FIGURE

○○○	?	F	E	F	F	E
	?	O	O	R	P	P
		a	b	c	d	(e)

5)

TEST FIGURE

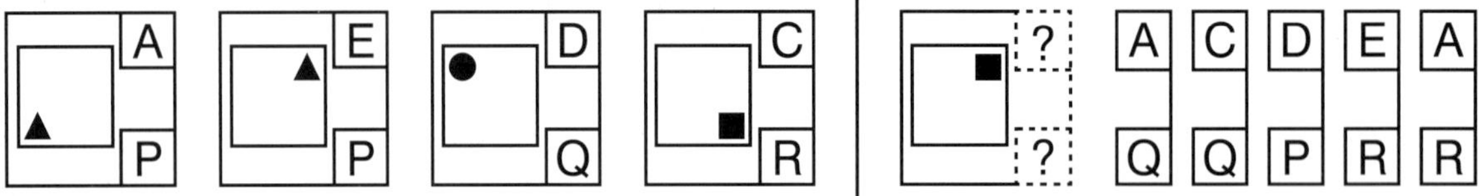

A	C	D	E	A
Q	Q	P	R	R

a   b   c   (d)   e

6)

TEST FIGURE

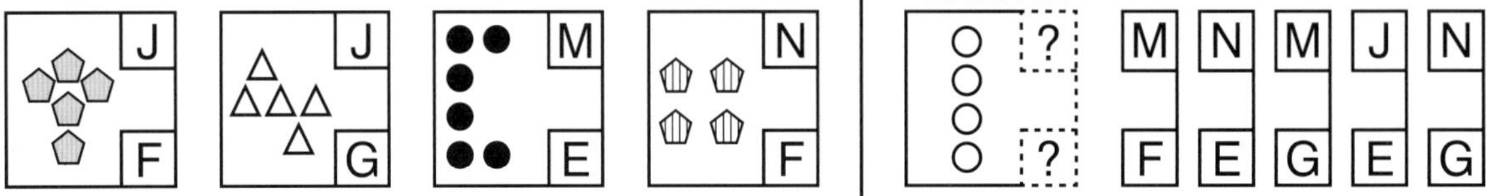

M	N	M	J	N
F	E	G	E	G

a   (b)   c   d   e

7)

TEST FIGURE

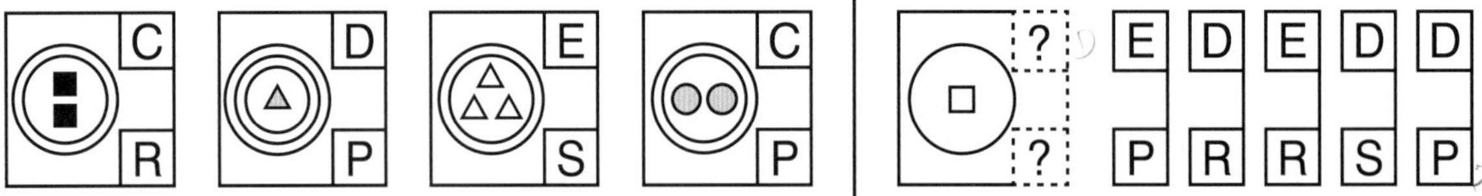

E	D	E	D	D
P	R	R	S	P

a   b   c   (d)   e

8)

TEST FIGURE

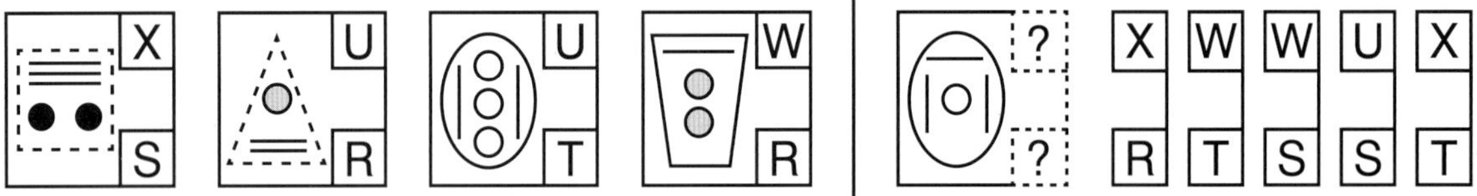

X	W	W	U	X
R	T	S	S	T

a   b   c   d   (e)

9)

TEST FIGURE

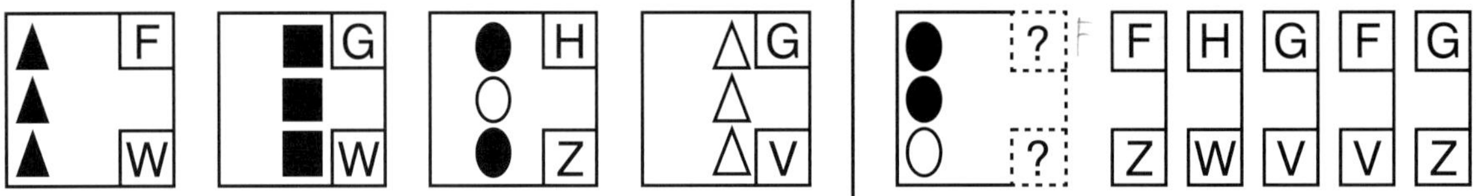

F	H	G	F	G
Z	W	V	V	Z

(a)   b   c   d   e

10)

TEST FIGURE

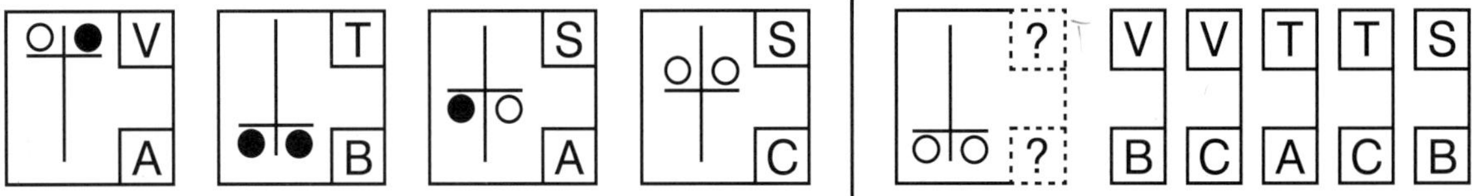

V	V	T	T	S
B	C	A	C	B

a   b   c   (d)   e

Score 9/10

Non-verbal Reasoning Test 2
Section A

On the left of each row are two figures with an arrow between them. Decide how the second figure is related to the first. After these there is a third figure, then an arrow and then five more figures. Decide which of the five figures goes with the third figure to make a pair like the two figures on the left.

Example

a   b   c   (d)   e

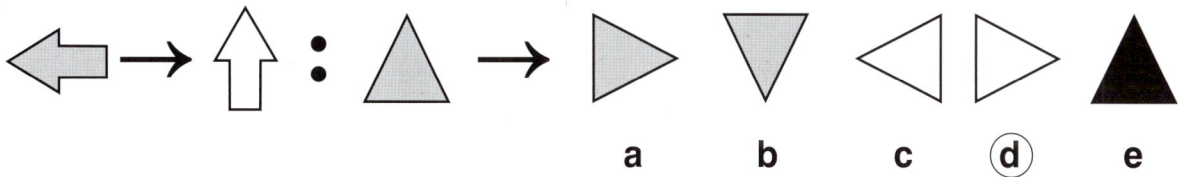

Now do the questions below. Circle the correct answer.

1)

a   b   c   d   (e)

2)

a   b   c   (d)   e

3)

a   (b)   c   d   e

4)

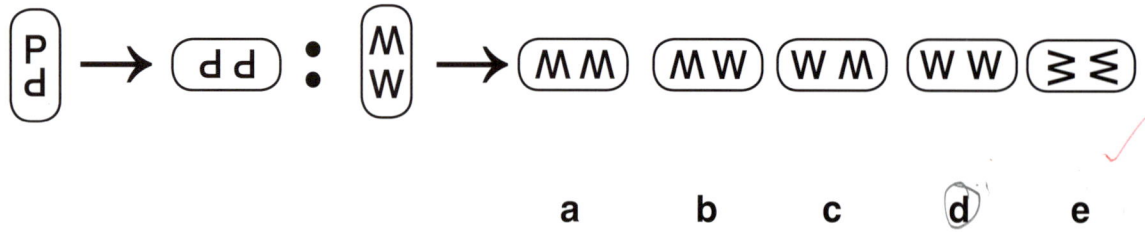

| | a | b | c | d | e |

5)

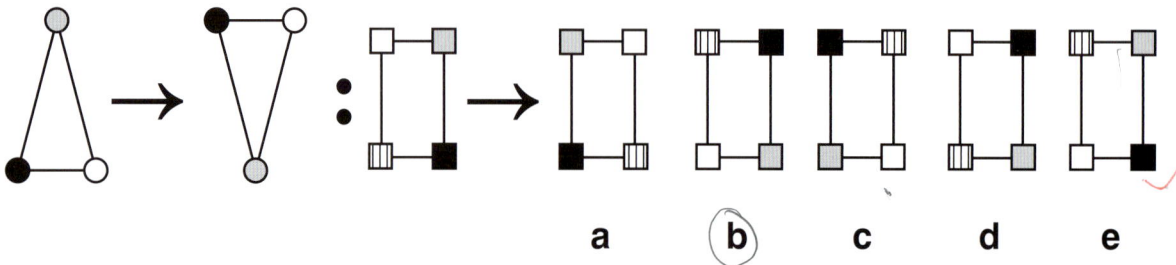

| | a | b | c | d | e |

6)

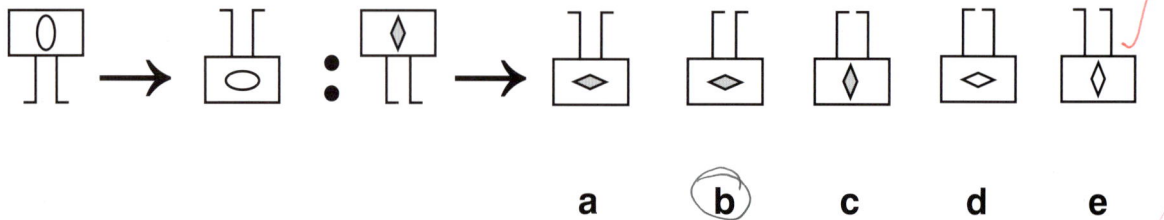

| | a | b | c | d | e |

7)

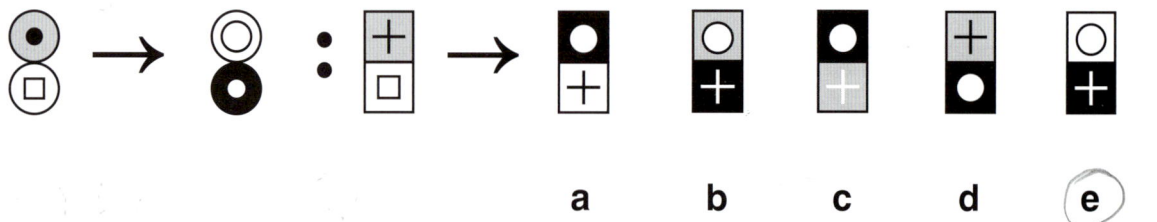

| | a | b | c | d | e |

8)

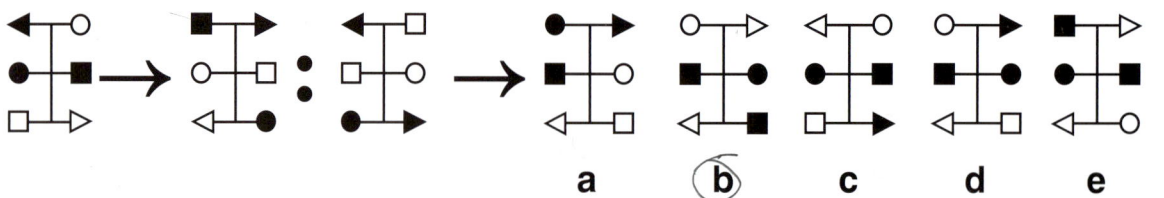

| | a | b | c | d | e |

Score

Section B

In each of the rows below there are five figures. Find one figure in each row that is **most unlike** the other four.

Example

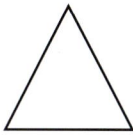   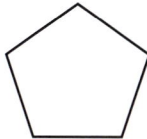   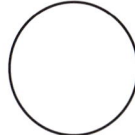   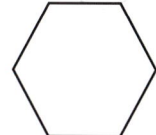

a   b   c   (d)   e

Now do the questions below. Circle the correct answer.

1)

   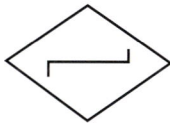   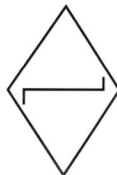   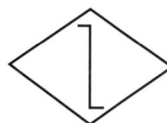   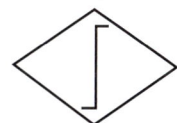

a   b   c   d   (e)

2)

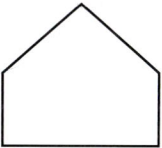   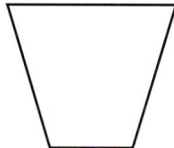   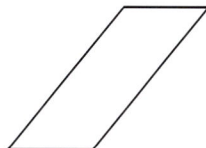   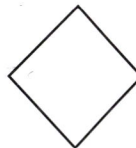   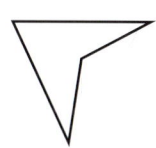

(a)   b   c   d   e

3)

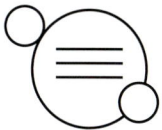   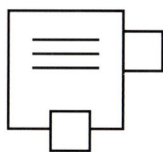         

a   b   (c)   (d)   e

4)

         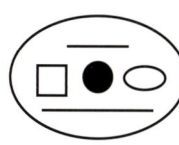   

a   b   (c)   d   e

5)

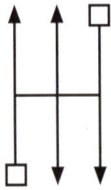 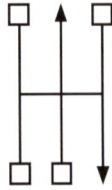   

a   b   c   d   e

6)

  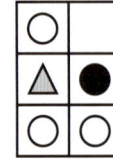

a   b   c   d   e

7)

  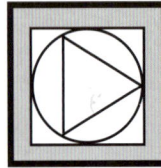 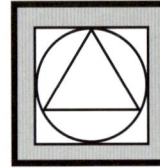 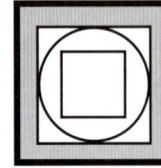

a   b   c   d   e

8)

   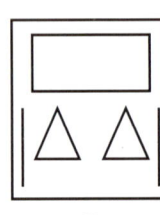 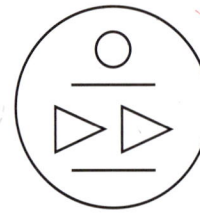

a   b   c   d   e

9)

 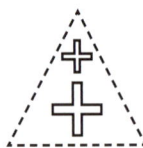 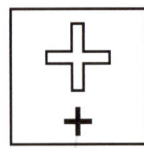  

a   b   c   d   e

Score

Section C

The following figures correspond to the codes next to them. You must decide how the code letters go with the figures and then find the correct code for the Test Figure.

Example

		TEST FIGURE	CZ	BY	AY	BZ	AZ
●	AZ		a	b	c	d	e
■	BZ						
▲	CY						

Now do the questions below. Circle the correct answer.

1)

		TEST FIGURE	AQ	CQ	BQ	CR	AR
	CQ		a	b	c	d	e
	BR						
	AQ						

2)

		TEST FIGURE	HB	GC	GA	HA	GB
	GA		a	b	c	d	e
	GB						
	HC						

3)

		TEST FIGURE	MA	KD	MC	KA	LC
	MD		a	b	c	d	e
	LA						
	KC						
	MB						

4)

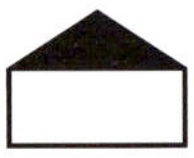

		WDR	VDQ	WCQ	VAR	VCR
	TEST FIGURE	(a)	b	c	d	e

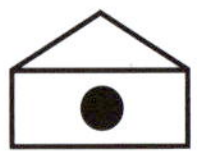

VDQ

WAR

VCR

5)

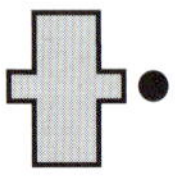

		NH	NG	MG	OG	MH
	TEST FIGURE	a	b	(c)	d	e

MH

NG

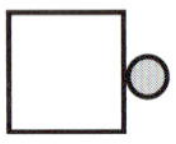

OH

6)

		KGC	HFA	JGC	JFA	HGC
	TEST FIGURE	(a)	b	c	d	e

HFC

KFB

JGB

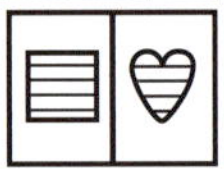

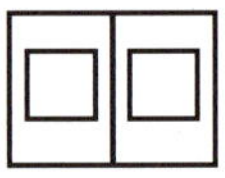

HGA

7)

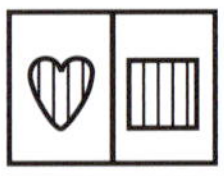

		VC	TC	SE	VD	TD
	TEST FIGURE	(a)	b	c	d	e

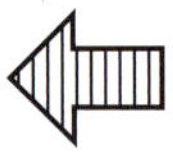

SC

TE

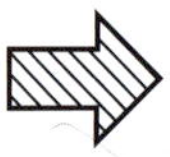

SD

VF

8)

		EJ	FJ	EK	GL	DJ
	TEST FIGURE	(a)	b	c	d	e

DJ

FK

EL

GJ

Score

Section D

On the left of each of the rows below there are two figures that are alike. On the right there are five more figures. Find which one of these five is **most like** the two figures on the left.

Example

a   b   c   d   e

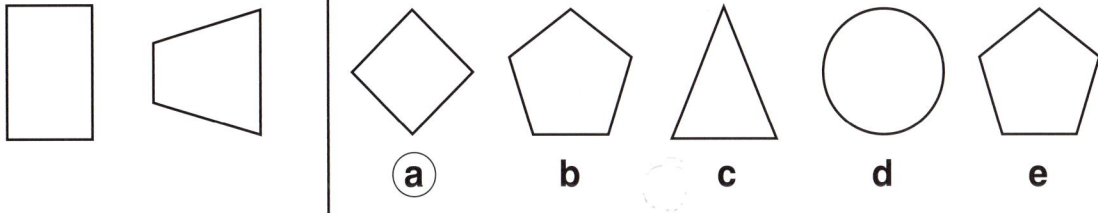

Now do the questions below. Circle the correct answer.

1)

a   b   c   d   e

2)

a   b   c   d   e

3)

a   b   c   d   e

4)

a   b   c   d   e

5)

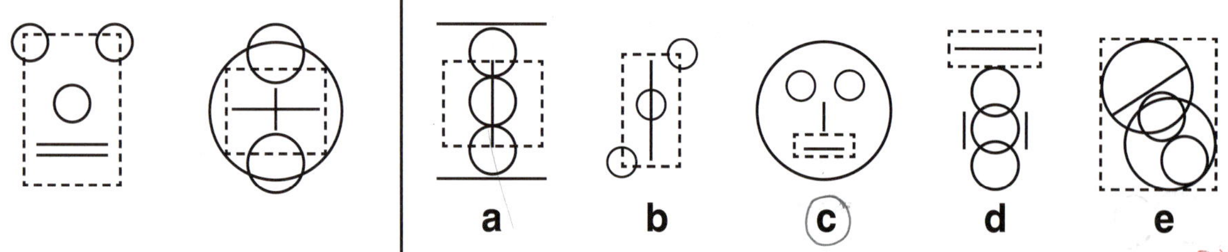

a   b   (c)   d   e

6)

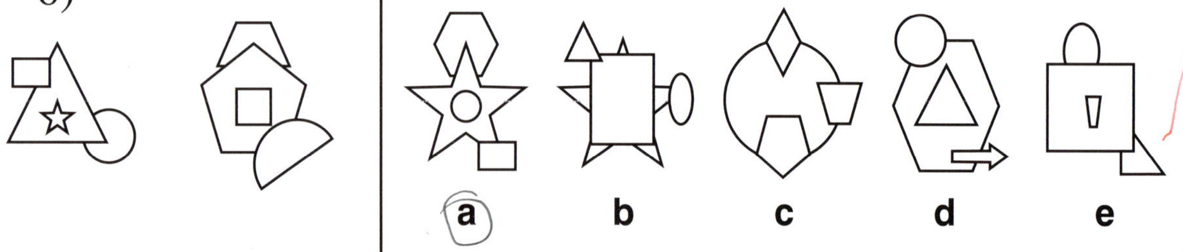

(a)   b   c   d   e

7)

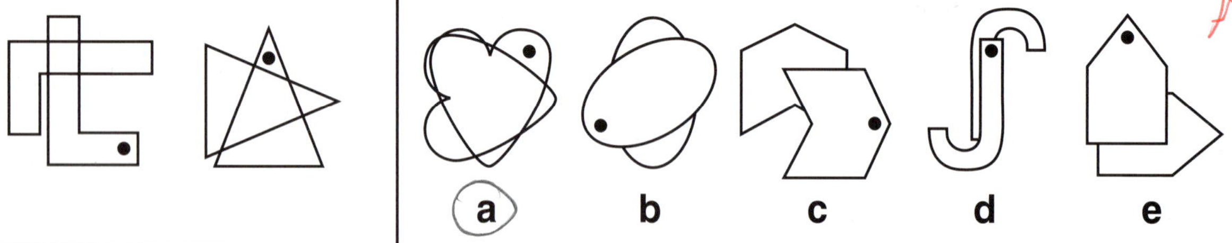

(a)   b   c   d   e

8)

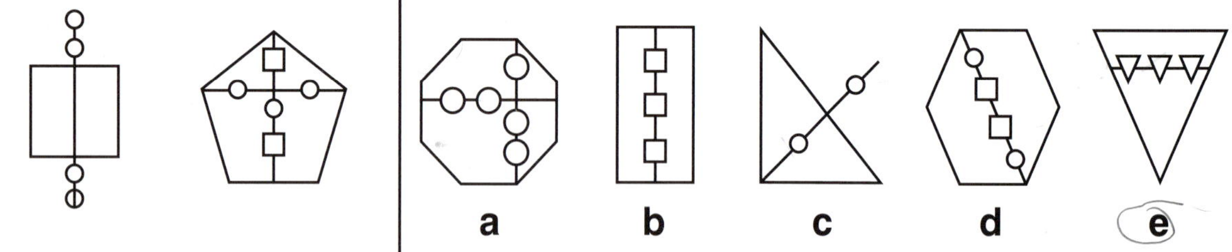

a   b   c   d   (e)

9)

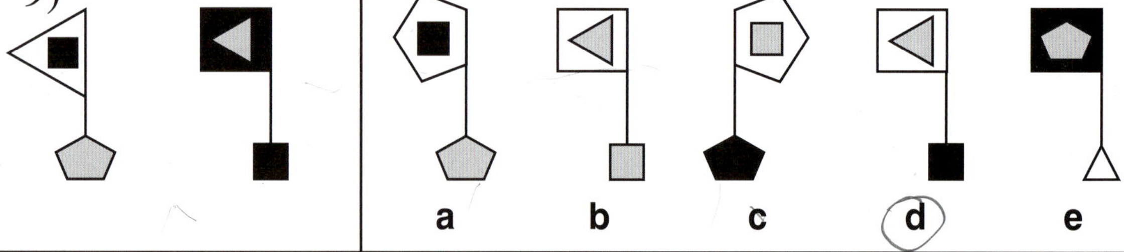

a   b   c   (d)   e

10)

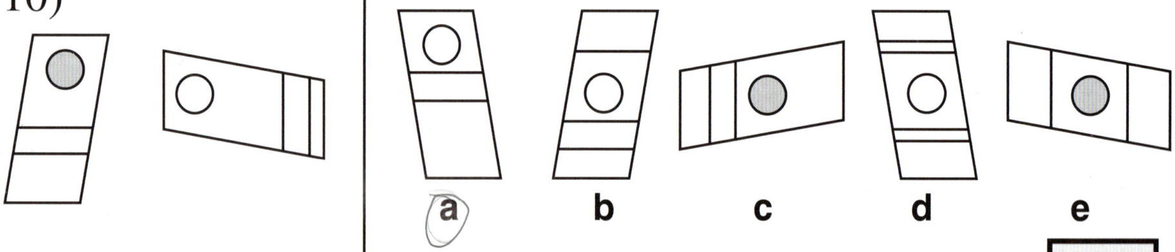

(a)   b   c   d   e

Score

Non-verbal Reasoning Test 3
Section A

The following figures correspond to the codes next to them. You must decide how the code letters go with the figures and then find the correct code for the Test Figure.

Example

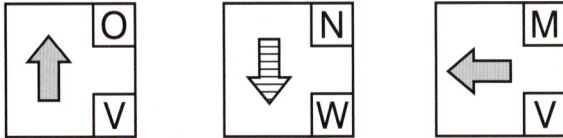

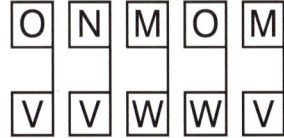

Now do the questions below. Circle the correct answer.

1)

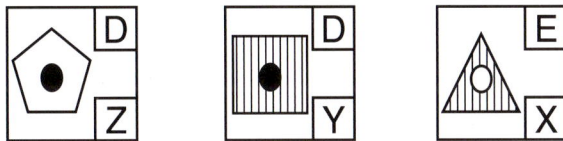

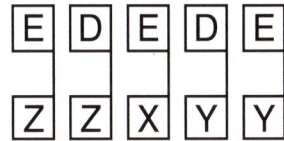

2)

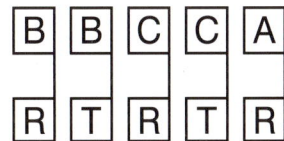

3)

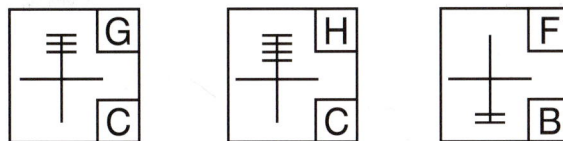

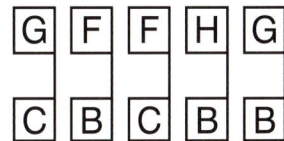

4)

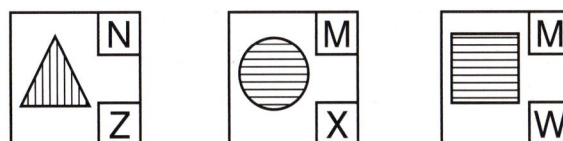

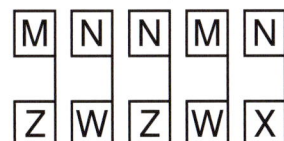

5)

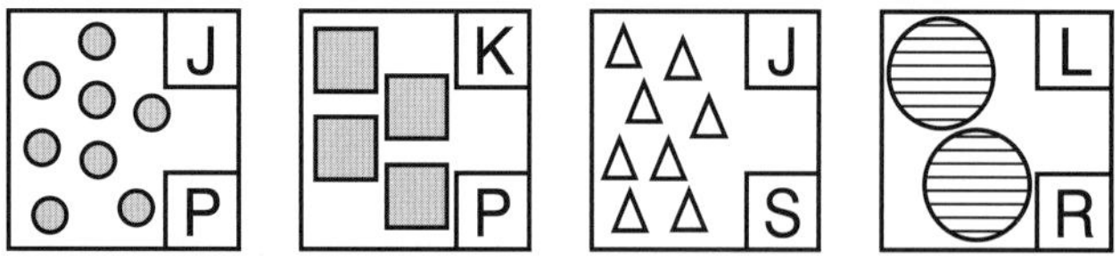

TEST FIGURE

	K	L	J	J	K
	S	P	P	S	R

a b c **d** e

6)

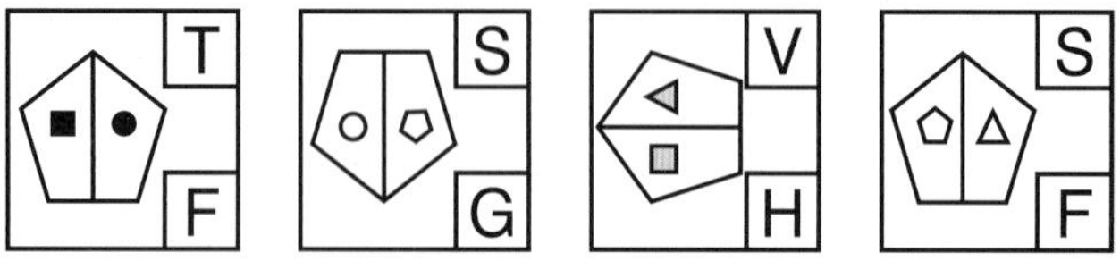

TEST FIGURE

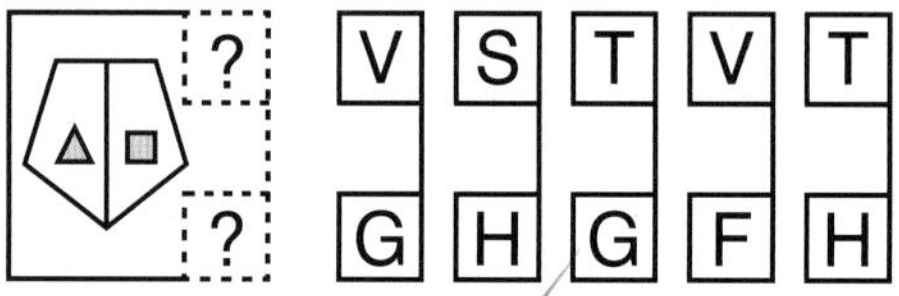

	V	S	T	V	T
	G	H	G	F	H

a b c d e

7)

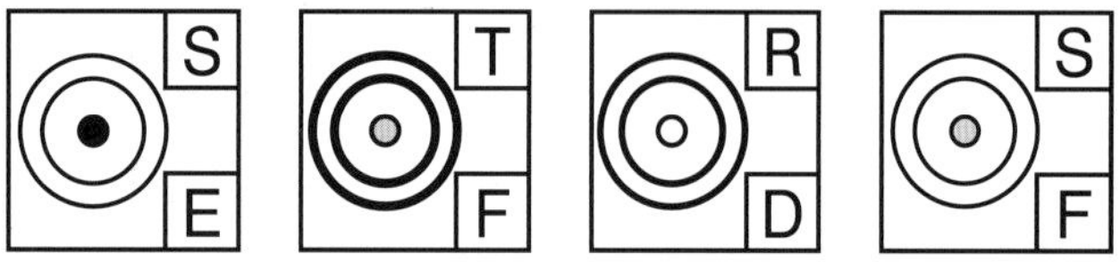

TEST FIGURE

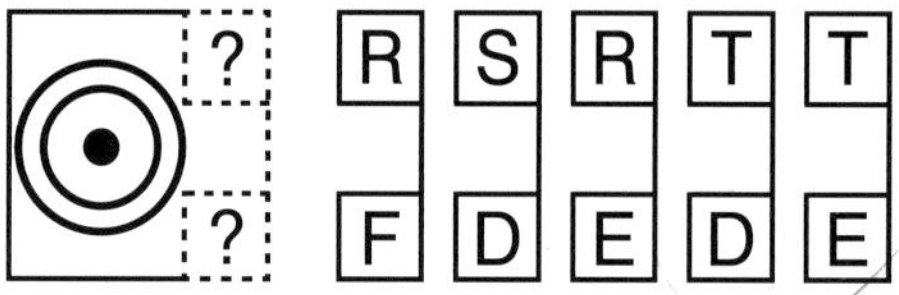

	R	S	R	T	T
	F	D	E	D	E

a b **c** d e

8)

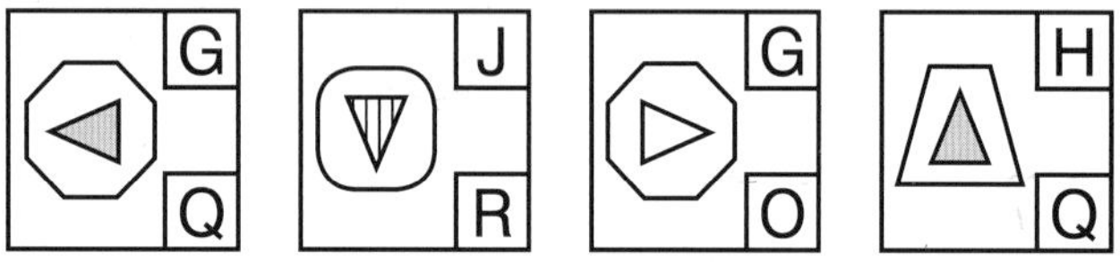

TEST FIGURE

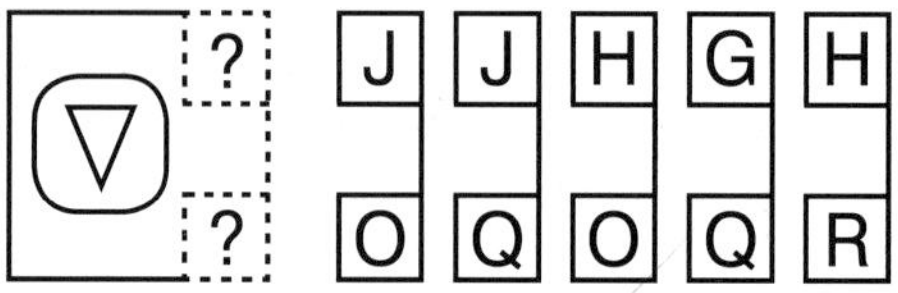

	J	J	H	G	H
	O	Q	O	Q	R

a b c d e

9)

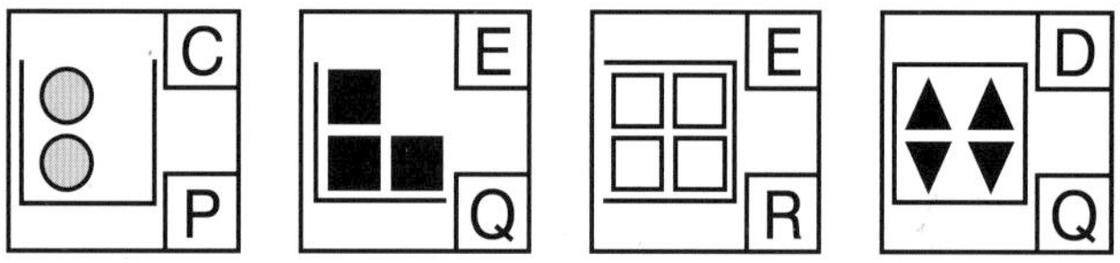

TEST FIGURE

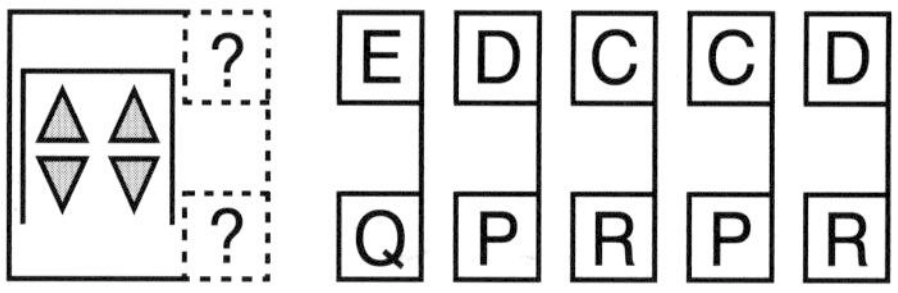

	E	D	C	C	D
	Q	P	R	P	R

a b c d e

Score 8

Section B

In the big square on the left of each line below, one of the small squares has been left empty. One of the five figures on the right should fill the empty square. Find this figure.

Example

Now do the questions below. Circle the correct answer.

1)

2)

3)

4)

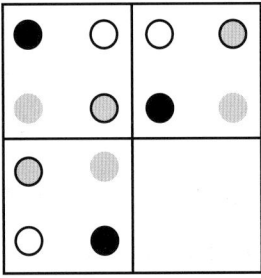 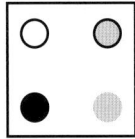 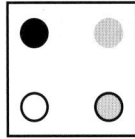 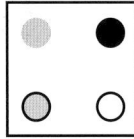 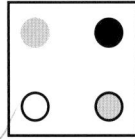 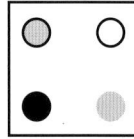

                   a   **b**   **c**   **d**   **e**

5)

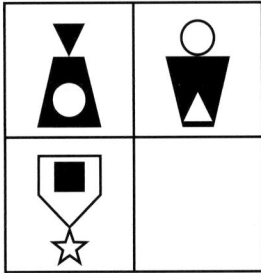   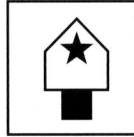 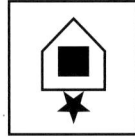 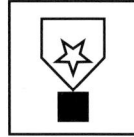

                   a   **b**   **c**   **d**   **e**

6)

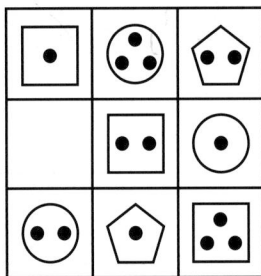 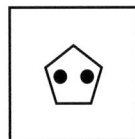 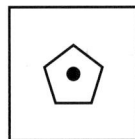 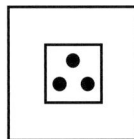  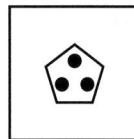

                   a   **b**   **c**   **d**   **e**

7)

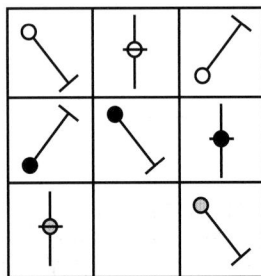

                   a   **b**   **c**   **d**   **e**

8)

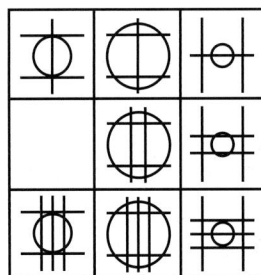

                   a   **b**   **c**   **d**   **e**

Score

Section C

To the left of each of the lines below there are five squares arranged in order. One of these squares has been left empty. Find which one of the five squares on the right should take the place of the empty square.

Example

a b c d e

Now do the questions below. Circle the correct answer.

1)

a b c d e

2)

a b c d e

3)

a b c d e

4)

a b c d e

5)

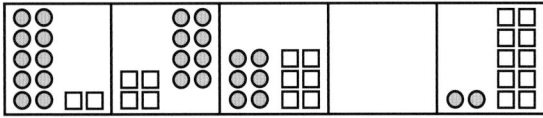 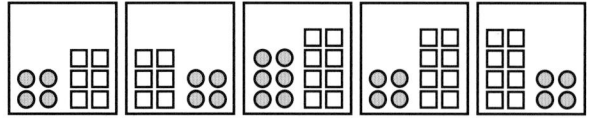

a **b** **c** **d** **e**

6)

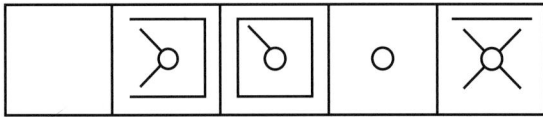 

a **b** **c** **d** **e**

7)

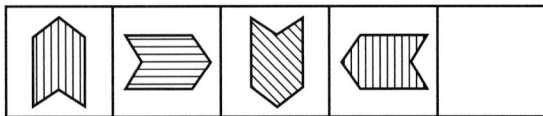 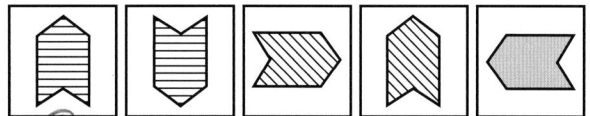

a **b** **c** **d** **e**

8)

 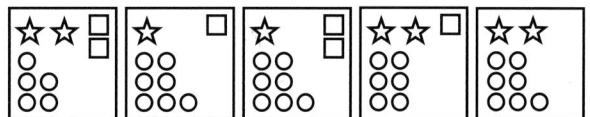

a **b** **c** **d** **e**

9)

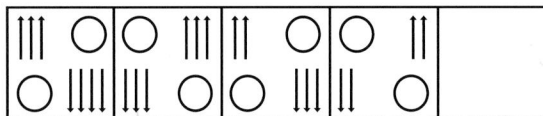 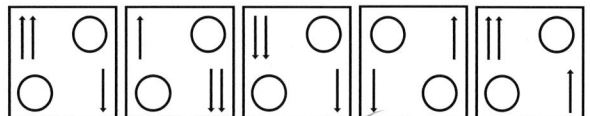

a **b** **c** **d** **e**

10)

 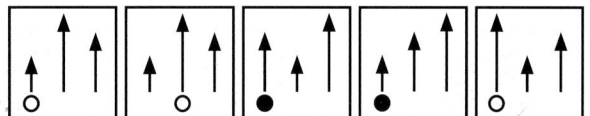

a **b** **c** **d** **e**

Score

Section D

In each of the rows below there are five figures. Find one figure in each row that is **most unlike** the other four.

Example

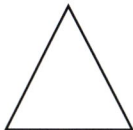 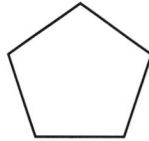 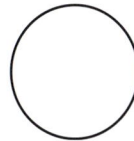 

a   b   c   d   e

Now do the questions below. Circle the correct answer.

1)

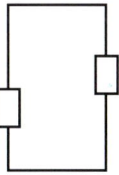  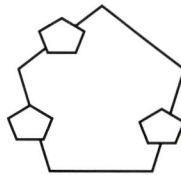 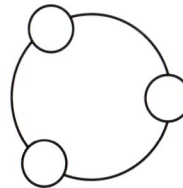 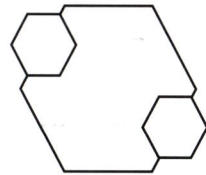

a   b   c   d   e

2)

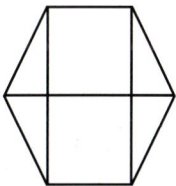 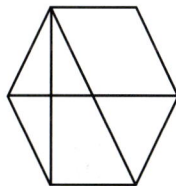  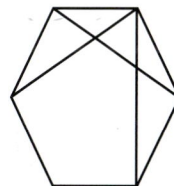 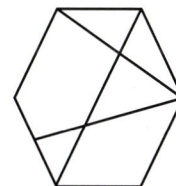

a   b   c   d   e

3)

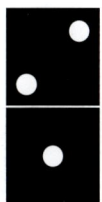 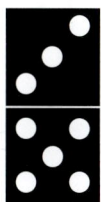 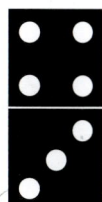 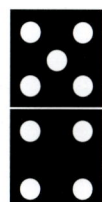 

a   b   c   d   e

4)

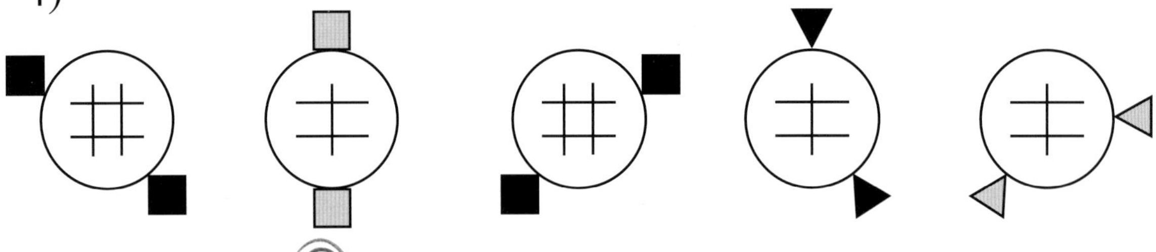

a   b   c   d   e

5)

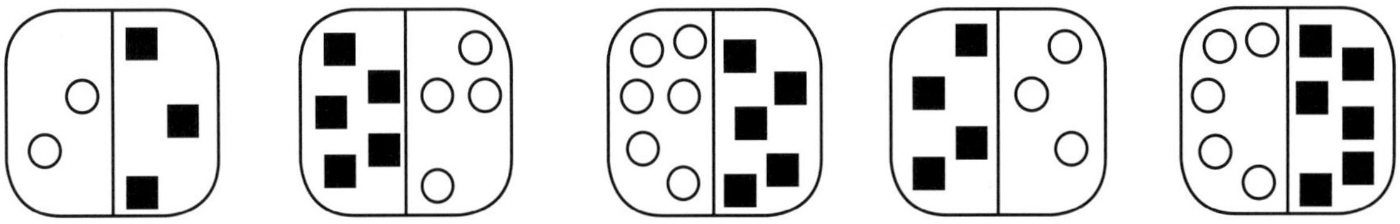

a   b   c   d   e

6)

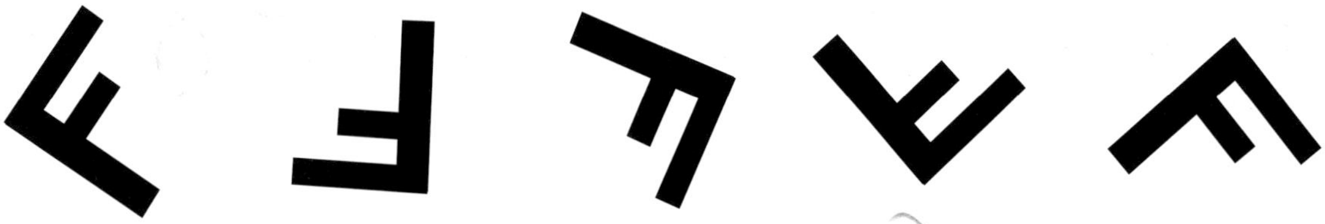

a   b   c   d   e

7)

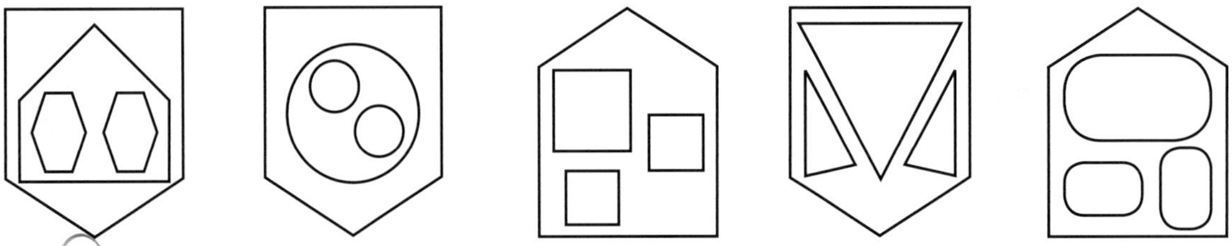

a   b   c   d   e

8)

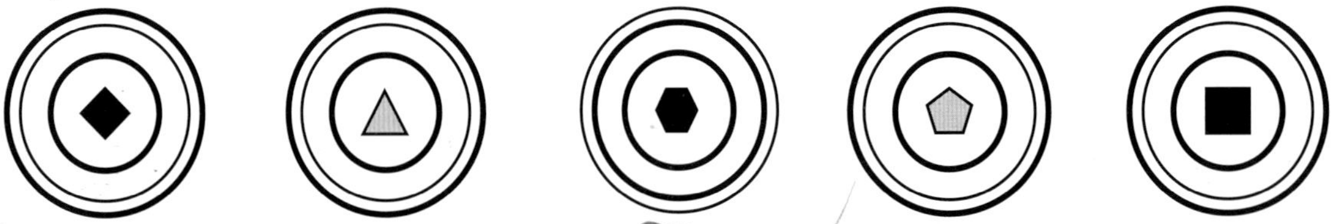

a   b   c   d   e

Score

Non-verbal Reasoning Test 4
Section A

On the left of each row are two figures with an arrow between them. Decide how the second figure is related to the first. After these there is a third figure, then an arrow and then five more figures. Decide which of the five figures goes with the third figure to make a pair like the two figures on the left.

Example

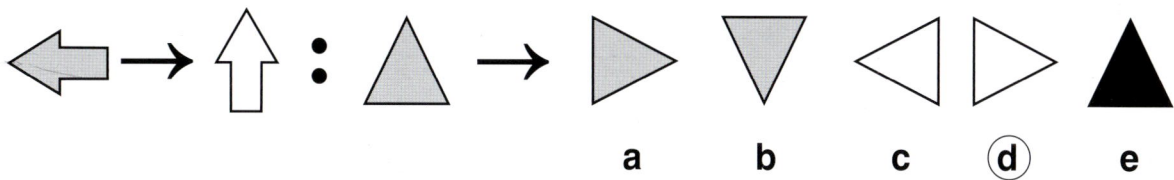

Now do the questions below. Circle the correct answer.

1)

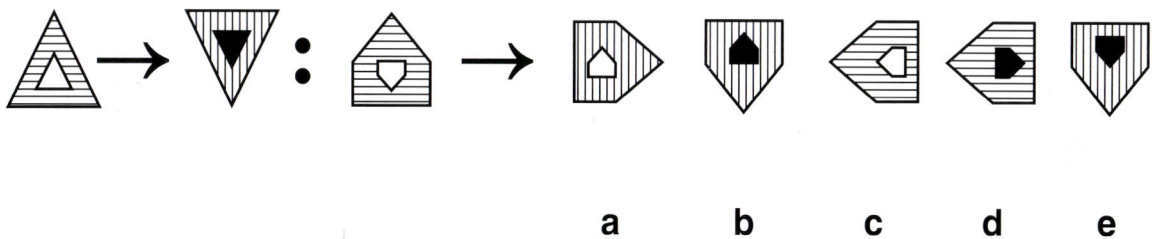

                a   b   c   d   e

2)

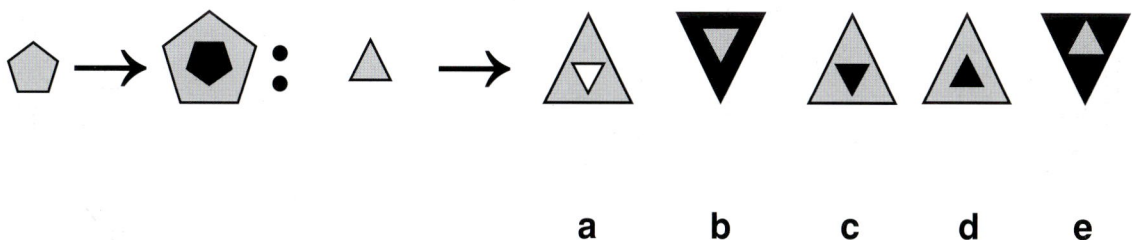

                a   b   c   d   e

3)

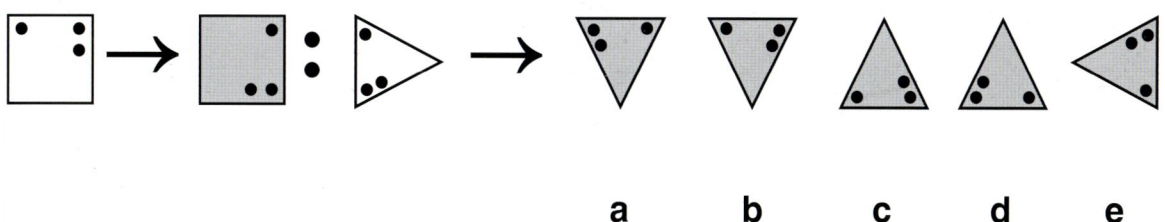

                a   b   c   d   e

4)

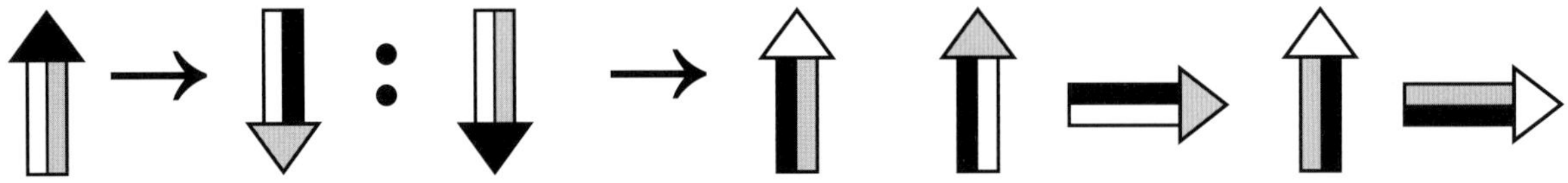

a   b   c   d   e

5)

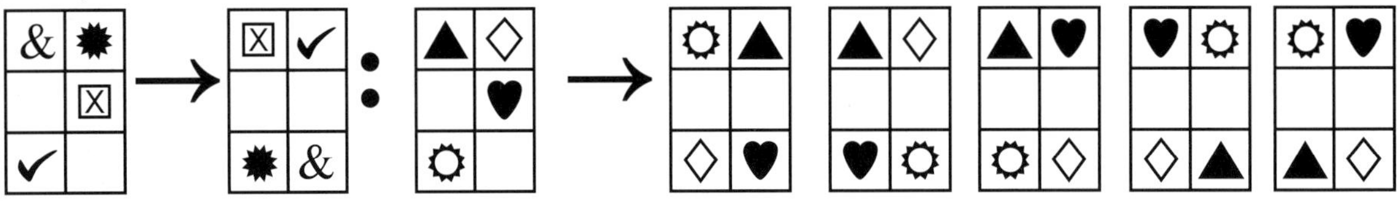

a   b   c   d   e

6)

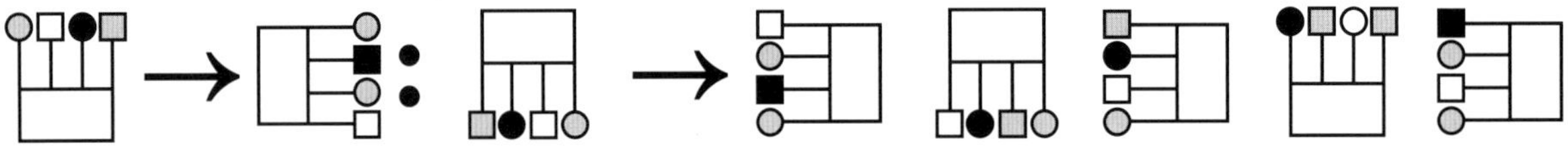

a   b   c   d   e

7)

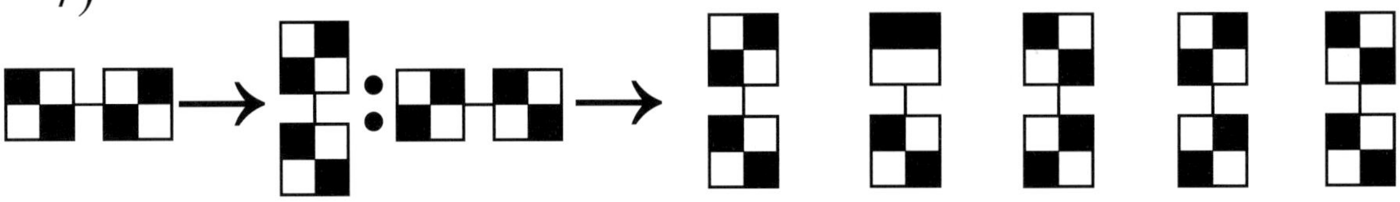

a   b   c   d   e

8)

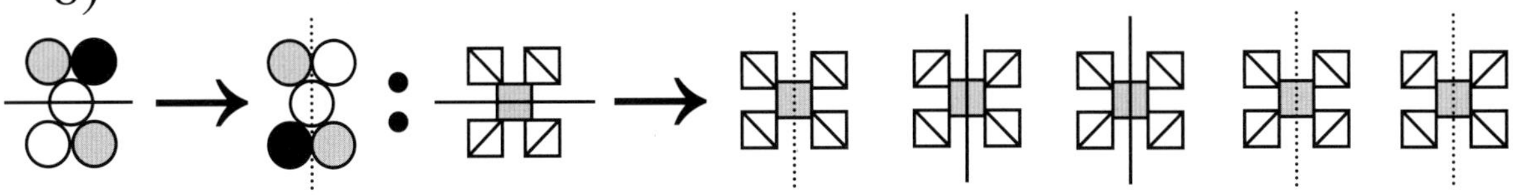

a   b   c   d   e

9)

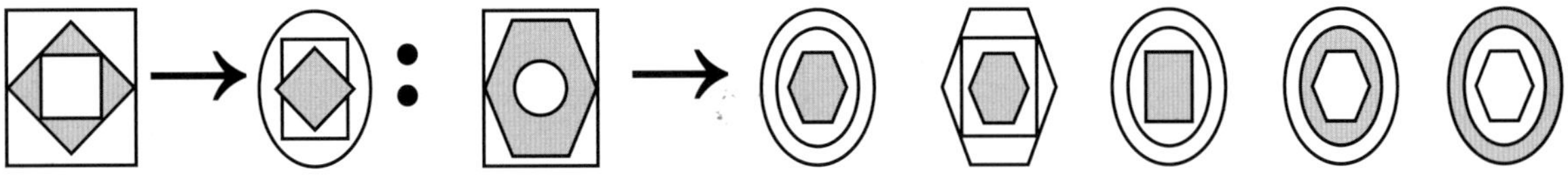

a   b   c   d   e

Score

Section B

In the big square on the left of each line below, one of the small squares has been left empty. One of the five figures on the right should fill the empty square. Find this figure.

Example

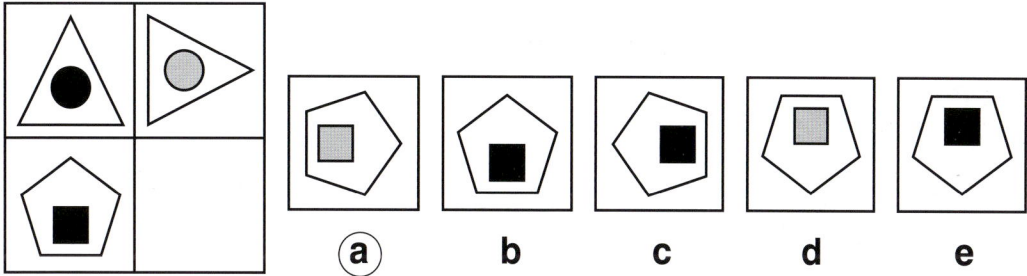

Now do the questions below. Circle the correct answer.

1)

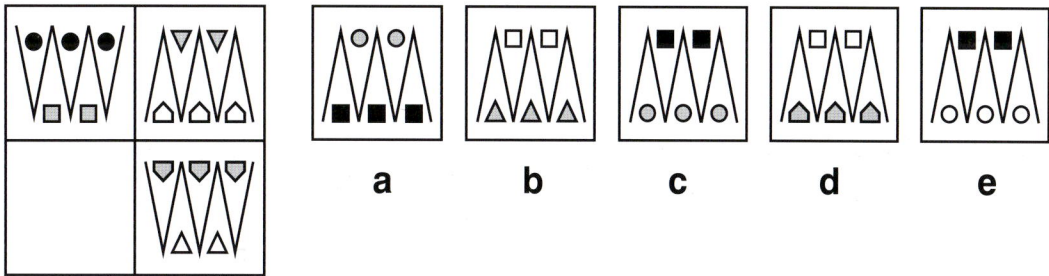

2)

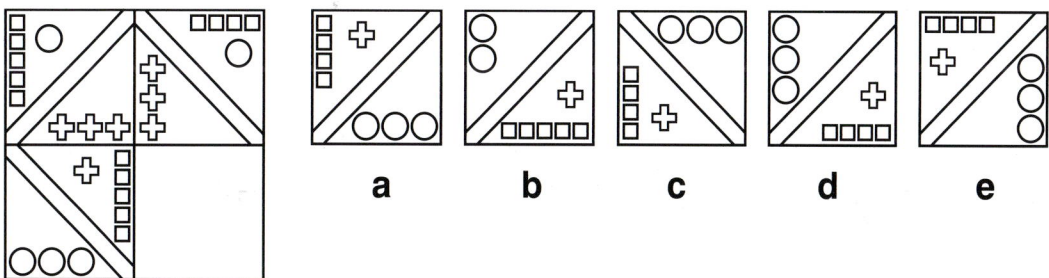

3)

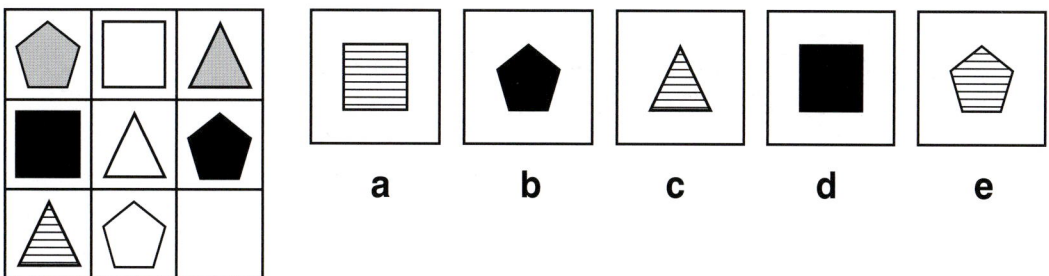

4)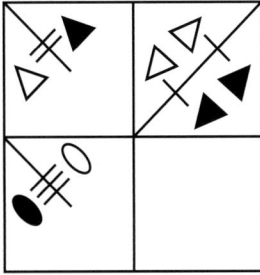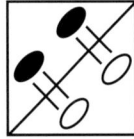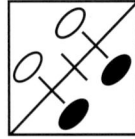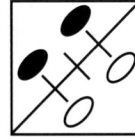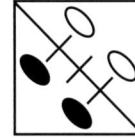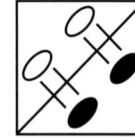

a   **b**   **c**   **d**   **e**

5)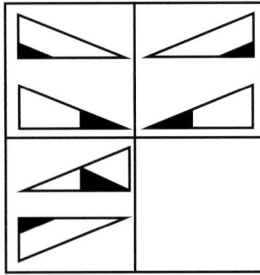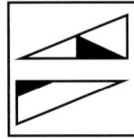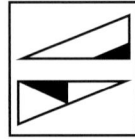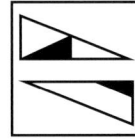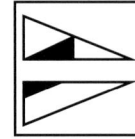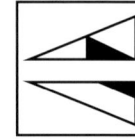

a   **b**   **c**   **d**   **e**

6)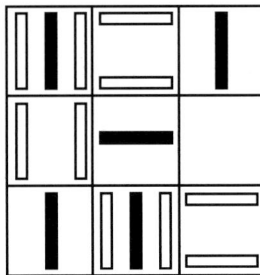

a   **b**   **c**   **d**   **e**

7)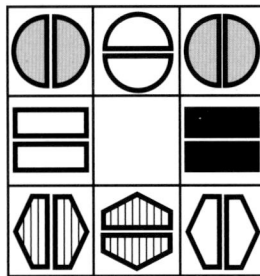

a   **b**   **c**   **d**   **e**

8)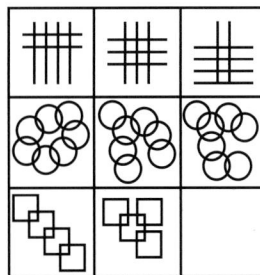

a   **b**   **c**   **d**   **e**

Score

Section C

The following figures correspond to the codes next to them. You must decide how the code letters go with the figures and then find the correct code for the Test Figure.

Example

● AZ					
■ BZ	TEST FIGURE	CZ **a**	BY **b**	AY **ⓒ**	BZ **d**	AZ **e**
△ CY						

Now do the questions below. Circle the correct answer.

1)

		HL	GL	GK	HM	HK
⬦ HK						
⬦ GM	TEST FIGURE	**a**	**b**	**c**	**d**	**e**
⬦ HL						

2)

		VZ	TZ	VX	TX	VW
◨ TW						
▯ TX	TEST FIGURE	**a**	**b**	**c**	**d**	**e**
▦ VZ						

3)

		BPH	BRG	CPG	CRH	CPH
●—■ BPG						
⬟—△ CPH	TEST FIGURE	**a**	**b**	**c**	**d**	**e**
△-----○ CRG						
□--⬟ BRH						

4)

		TEST FIGURE	QBY	QAY	PAX	PBY	PAZ
	PAY		a	b	c	d	e
	QAX						
	PBZ						

5)

		TEST FIGURE	YNB	ZNB	ZMC	YNC	XNC
	XMB		a	b	c	d	e
	ZNB						
	YMC						

6)

		TEST FIGURE	DPH	BRE	ARF	CPH	BPE
	DPF		a	b	c	d	e
	ARE						
	CPF						
	BRH						

7)

		TEST FIGURE	GSX	HRT	GTX	GRX	HTY
	GRX		a	b	c	d	e
	HSY						
	GTY						
	HRX						

8)

		TEST FIGURE	XP	YR	XQ	YP	YQ
	XP		a	b	c	d	e
	XQ						
	YR						
	YP						

Score

Section D

On the left of each of the rows below there are two figures that are alike. On the right there are five more figures. Find which one of these five is **most like** the two figures on the left.

Example

a   b   c   d   e

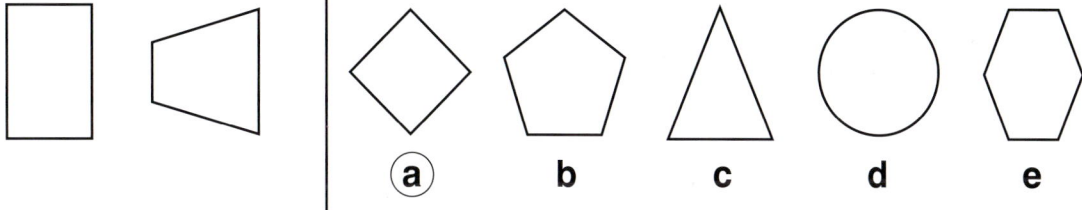

Now do the questions below. Circle the correct answer.

1)

a   b   c   d   e

2)

a   b   c   d   e

3)

a   b   c   d   e

4)

a   b   c   d   e

5)

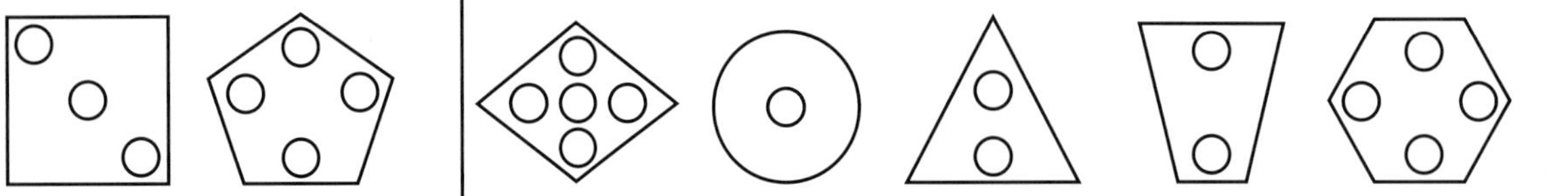

a   b   c   d   e

6)

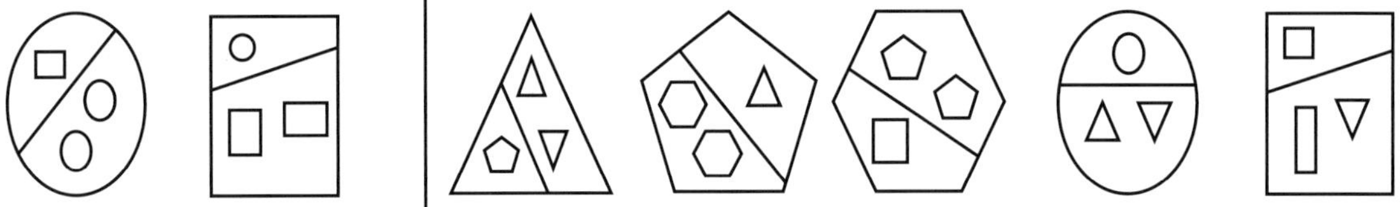

a   b   c   d   e

7)

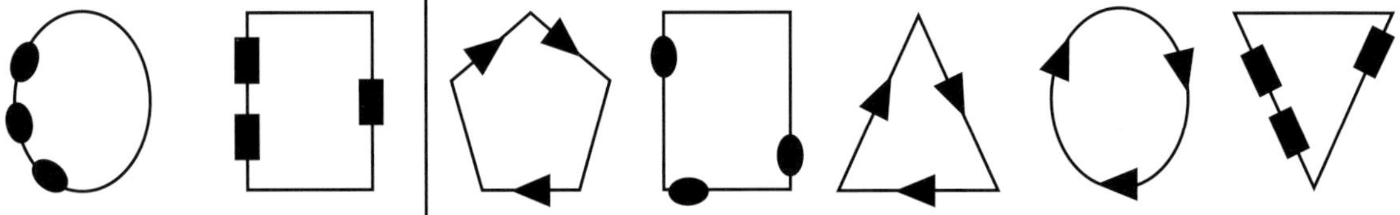

a   b   c   d   e

8)

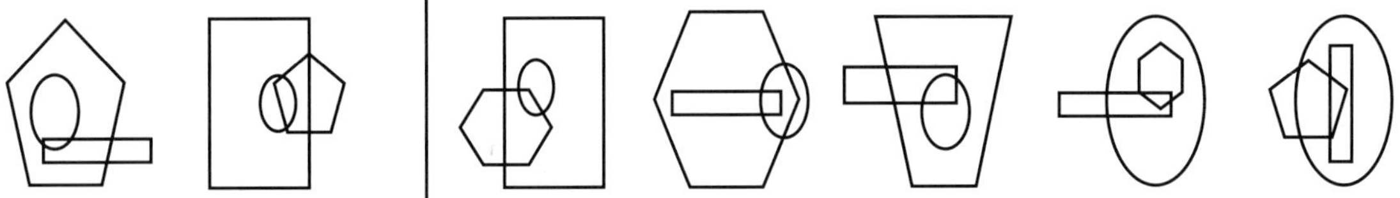

a   b   c   d   e

9)

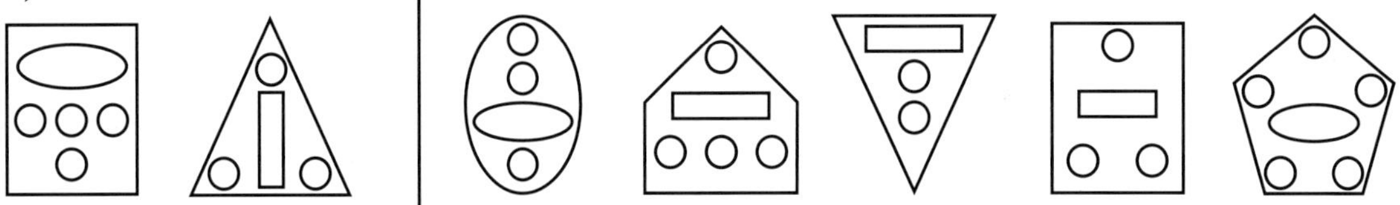

a   b   c   d   e

10)

a   b   c   d   e

Score

Non-verbal Reasoning Test 5
Section A

To the left of each of the lines below there are five squares arranged in order. One of these squares has been left empty. Find which one of the five squares on the right should take the place of the empty square.

Example

Now do the questions below. Circle the correct answer.

1)

2)

3)

4)

5)

 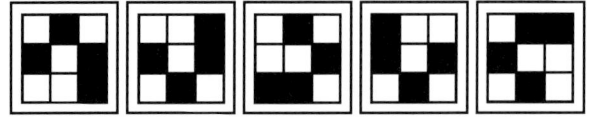

a **b** **c** **d** **e**

6)

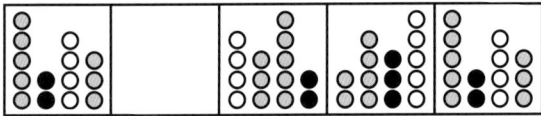 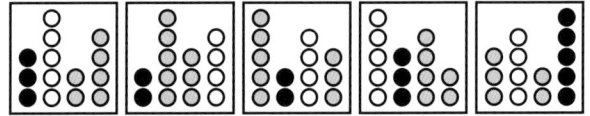

a **b** **c** **d** **e**

7)

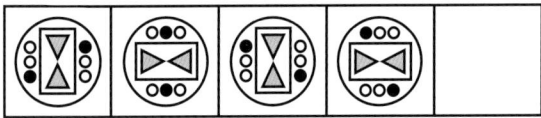 

a **b** **c** **d** **e**

8)

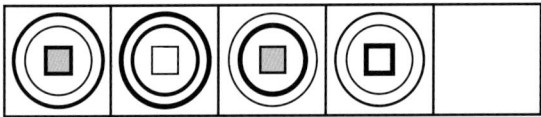 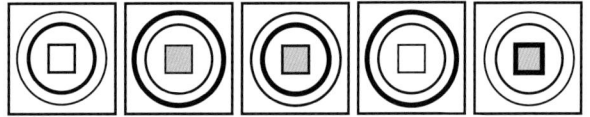

a **b** **c** **d** **e**

9)

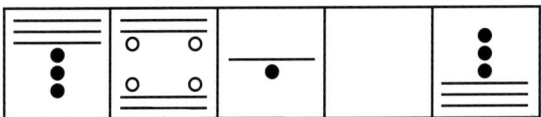 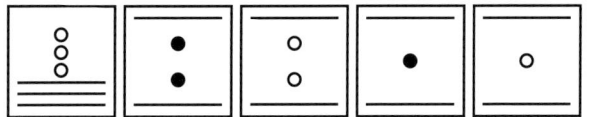

a **b** **c** **d** **e**

Score

Section B

On the left of each row are two figures with an arrow between them. Decide how the second figure is related to the first. After these there is a third figure, then an arrow and then five more figures. Decide which of the five figures goes with the third figure to make a pair like the two figures on the left.

Example

a   b   c   (d)   e

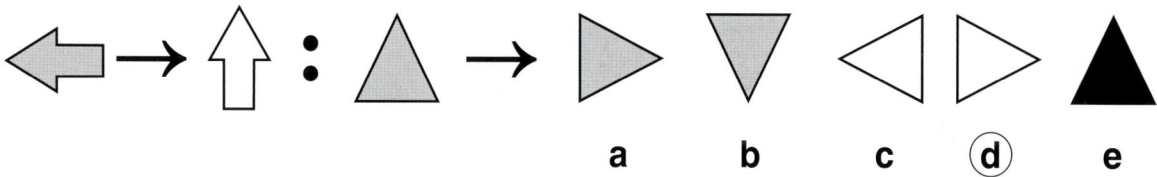

Now do the questions below. Circle the correct answer.

1)

a   b   c   d   e

2)

a   b   c   d   e

3)

a   b   c   d   e

4)

                                       a   **b**   **c**   **d**   **e**

5)

    a   **b**   **c**   **d**   **e**

6)

    a   **b**   **c**   **d**   **e**

7)

    a   **b**   **c**   **d**   **e**

8)

    a   **b**   **c**   **d**   **e**

Score

Section C

In each of the rows below there are five figures. Find one figure in each row that is **most unlike** the other four.

Example

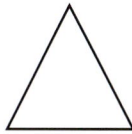   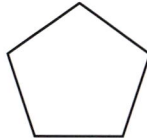   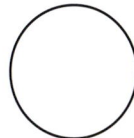   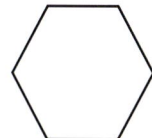

a   b   c   d   e

Now do the questions below. Circle the correct answer.

1)

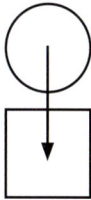            

a   b   c   d   e

2)

   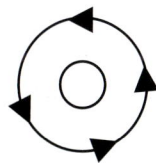   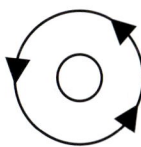   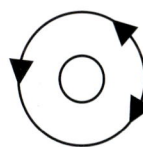   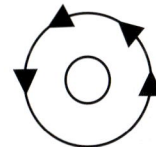

a   b   c   d   e

3)

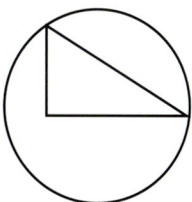   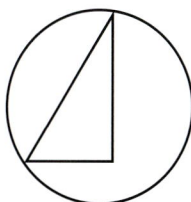   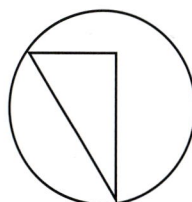   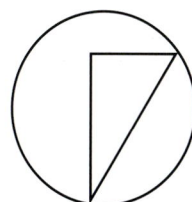   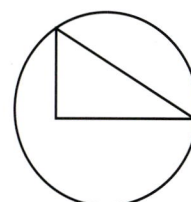

a   b   c   d   e

4)

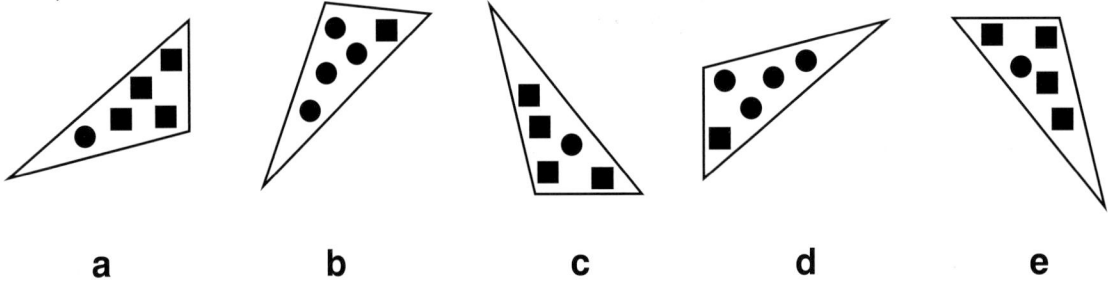

a　　**b**　　**c**　　**d**　　**e**

5)

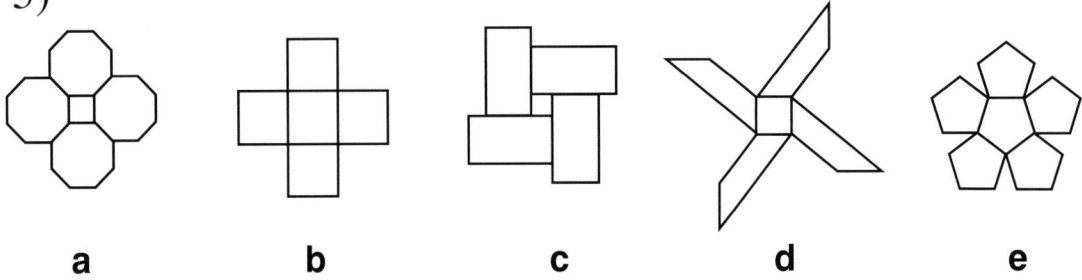

a　　**b**　　**c**　　**d**　　**e**

6)

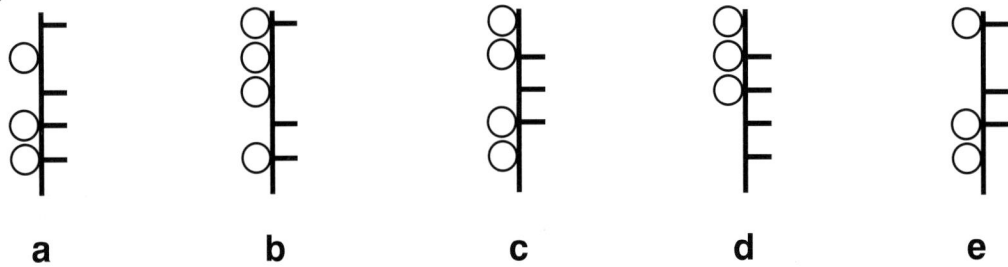

a　　**b**　　**c**　　**d**　　**e**

7)

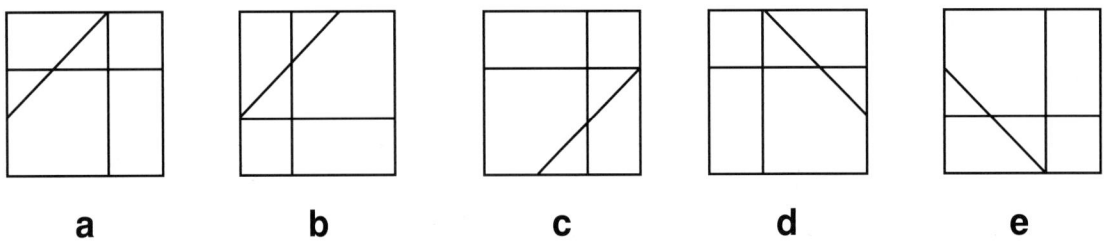

a　　**b**　　**c**　　**d**　　**e**

8)

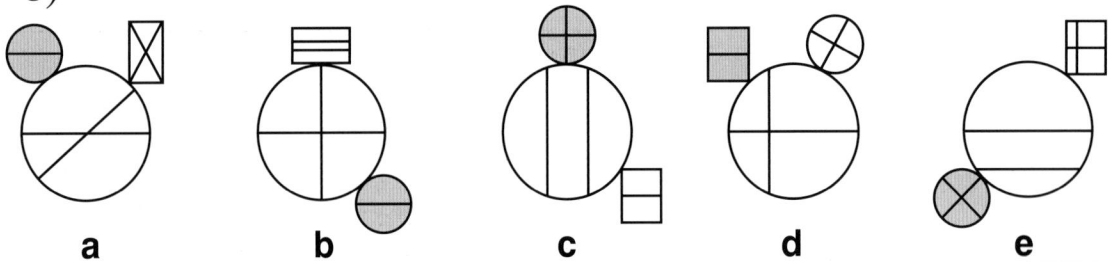

a　　**b**　　**c**　　**d**　　**e**

Score

Section D

The following figures correspond to the codes next to them. You must decide how the code letters go with the figures and then find the correct code for the Test Figure.

Example

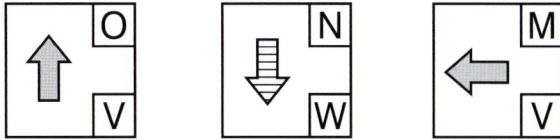

TEST FIGURE

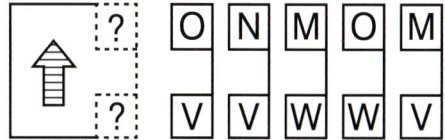

Now do the questions below. Circle the correct answer.

1)

TEST FIGURE

2)

TEST FIGURE

3)

TEST FIGURE

4)

TEST FIGURE

5)

TEST FIGURE

	A	D	B	A	B
	T	S	R	R	T
	a	b	c	d	e

6)

TEST FIGURE

	N	M	L	M	O
	R	S	S	T	R
	a	b	c	d	e

7)

TEST FIGURE

	S	R	S	P	R
	D	C	E	D	E
	a	b	c	d	e

8)

TEST FIGURE

	B	E	B	E	F
	L	L	K	M	K
	a	b	c	d	e

9)

TEST FIGURE

	F	G	H	G	H
	R	T	R	S	T
	a	b	c	d	e

10)

TEST FIGURE

	E	D	D	E	C
	K	J	M	L	M
	a	b	c	d	e

Score

Non-verbal Reasoning Test 6
Section A

On the left of each of the rows below there are two figures that are alike. On the right there are five more figures. Find which one of these five is **most like** the two figures on the left.

Example

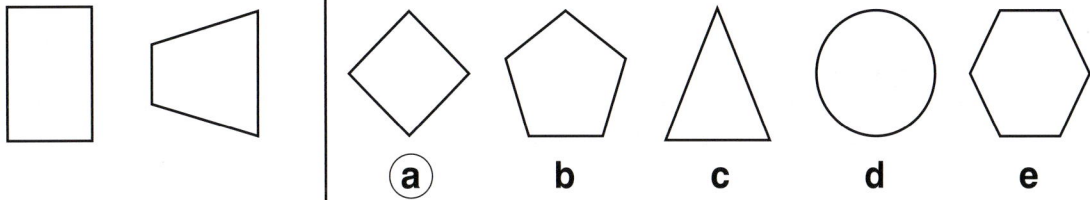

Now do the questions below. Circle the correct answer.

1)

a   b   c   d   e

2)

a   b   c   d   e

3)

a   b   c   d   e

4)

a   b   c   d   e

5)

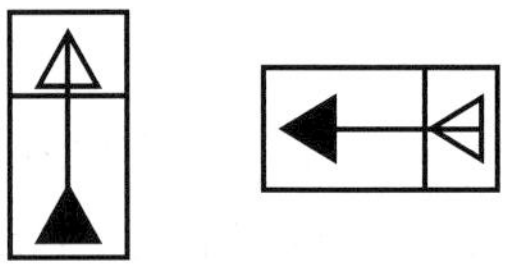

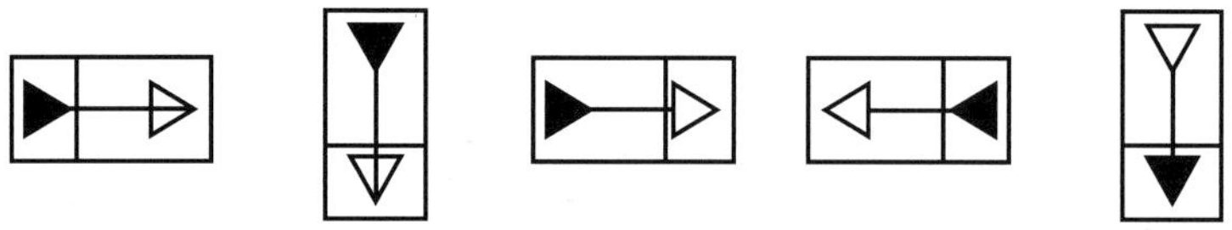

a   b   c   d   e

6)

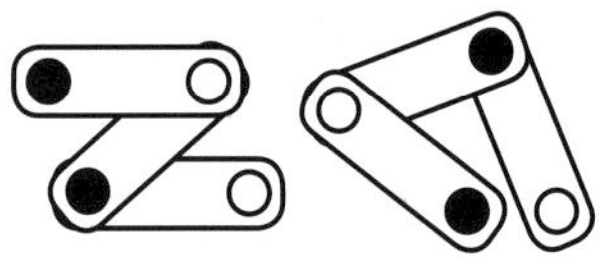

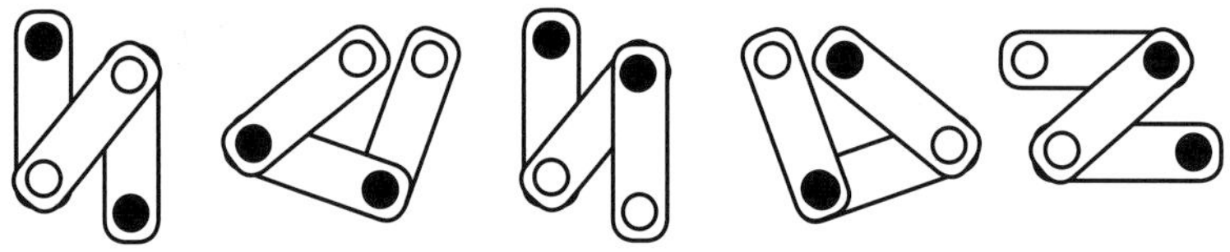

a   b   c   d   e

7)

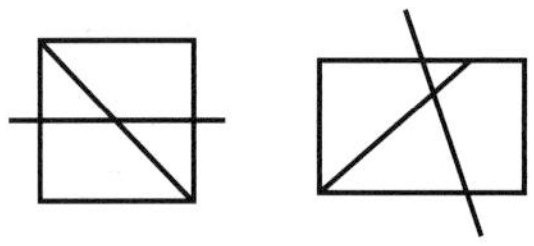

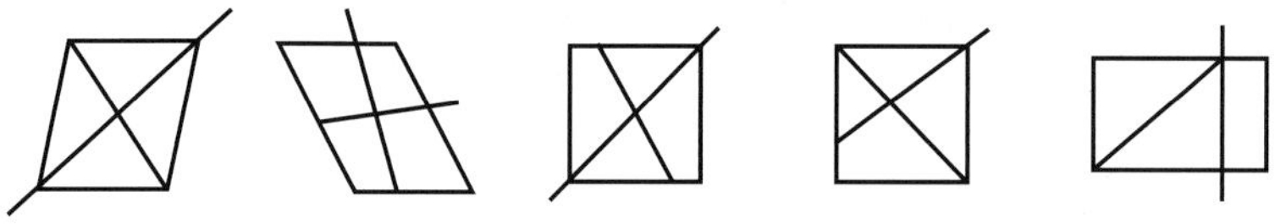

a   b   c   d   e

8)

a   b   c   d   e

9)

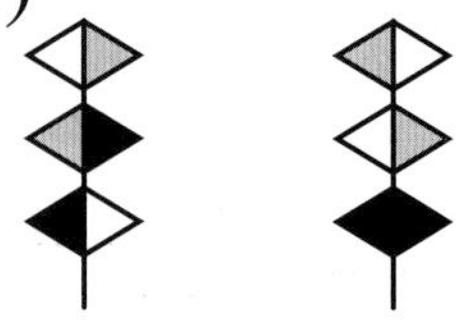

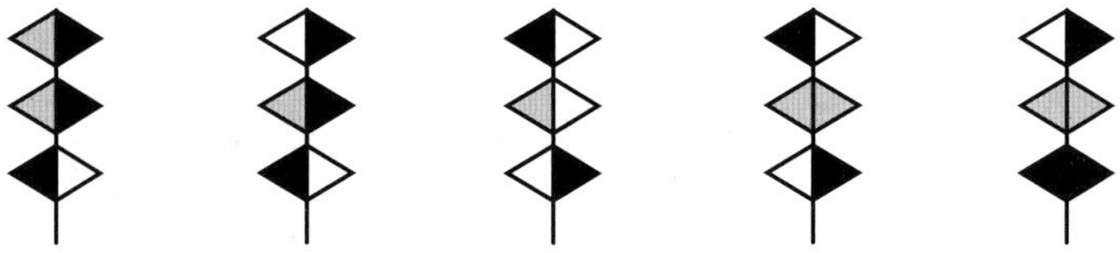

a   b   c   d   e

Score

Section B

In the big square on the left of each line below, one of the small squares has been left empty. One of the five figures on the right should fill the empty square. Find this figure.

Example

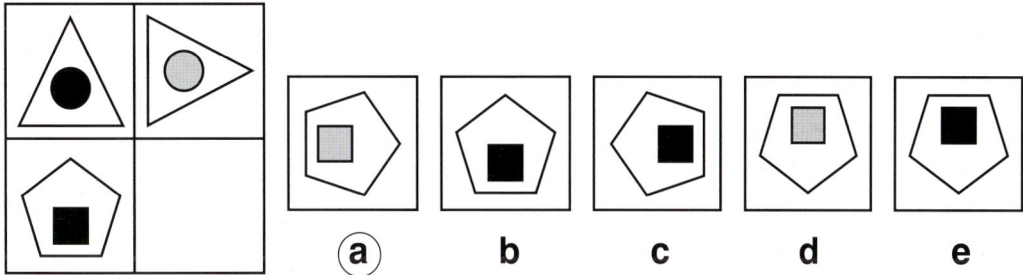

Now do the questions below. Circle the correct answer.

1)

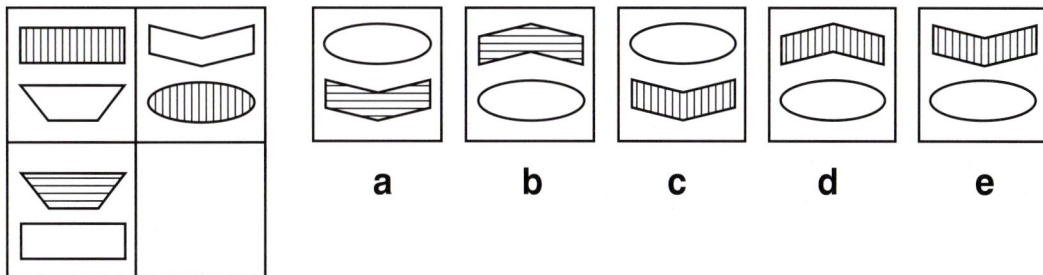

2)

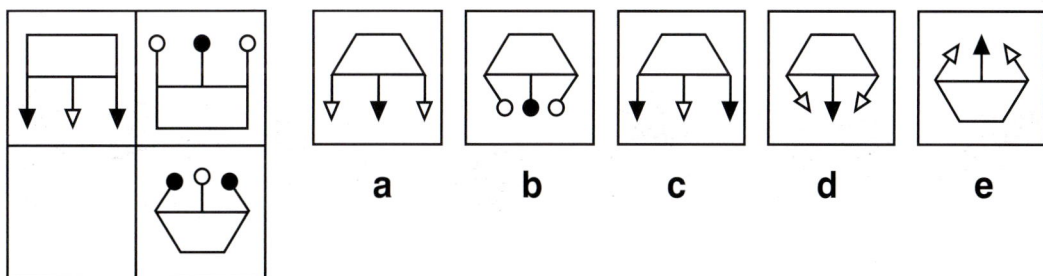

3)

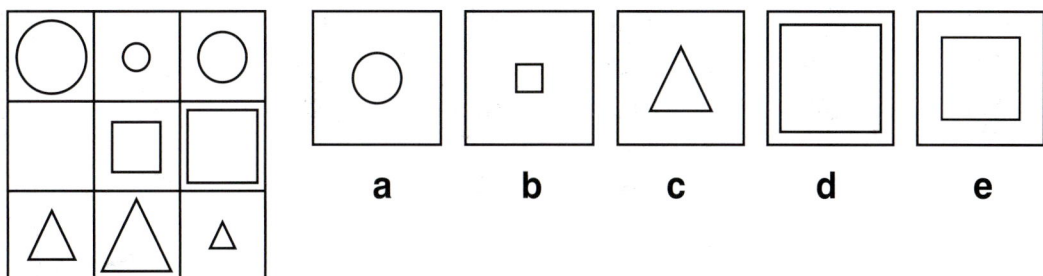

4) 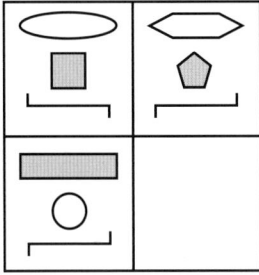   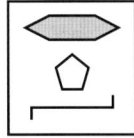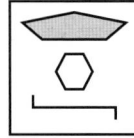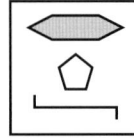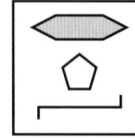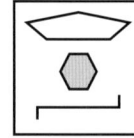

a   **b**   **c**   **d**   **e**

5) 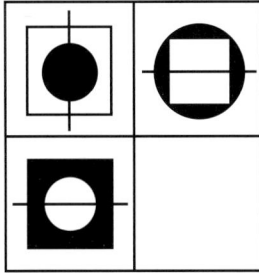   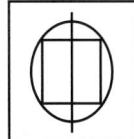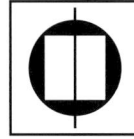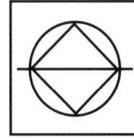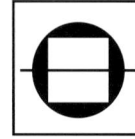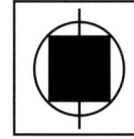

a   **b**   **c**   **d**   **e**

6)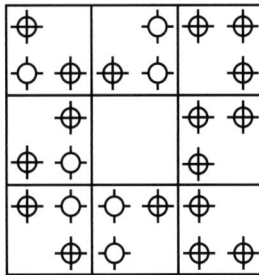

a   **b**   **c**   **d**   **e**

7)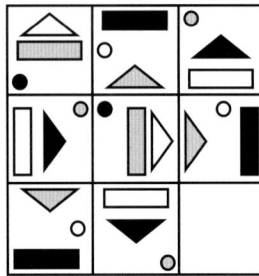

a   **b**   **c**   **d**   **e**

8)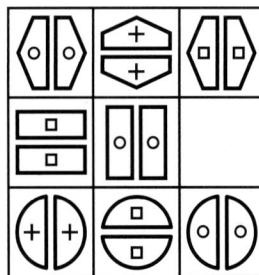

a   **b**   **c**   **d**   **e**

Score

Section C

To the left of each of the lines below there are five squares arranged in order. One of these squares has been left empty. Find which one of the five squares on the right should take the place of the empty square.

Example

a   (b)   c   d   e

Now do the questions below. Circle the correct answer.

1)

a   b   c   d   e

2)

a   b   c   d   e

3)

a   b   c   d   e

4)

a   b   c   d   e

5)

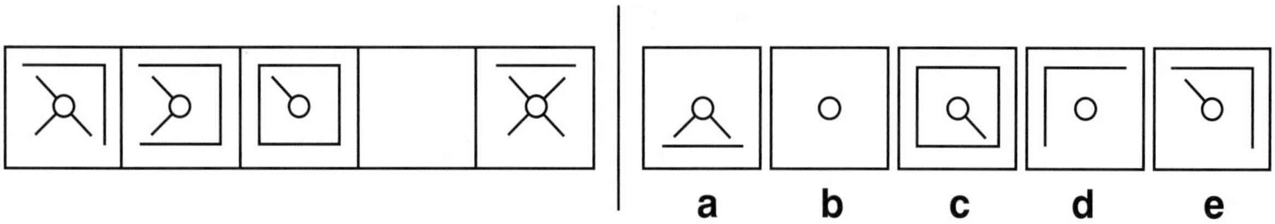

6)

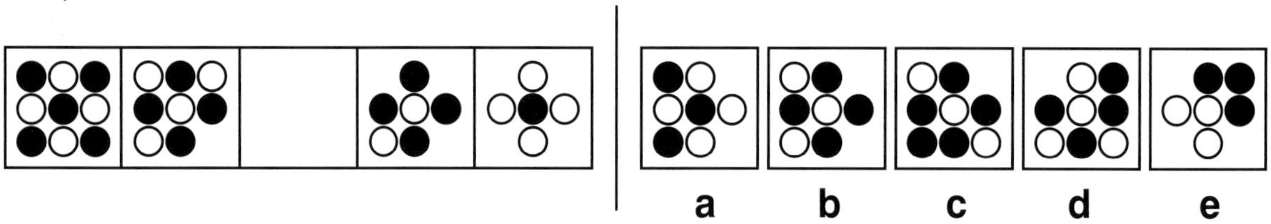

7)

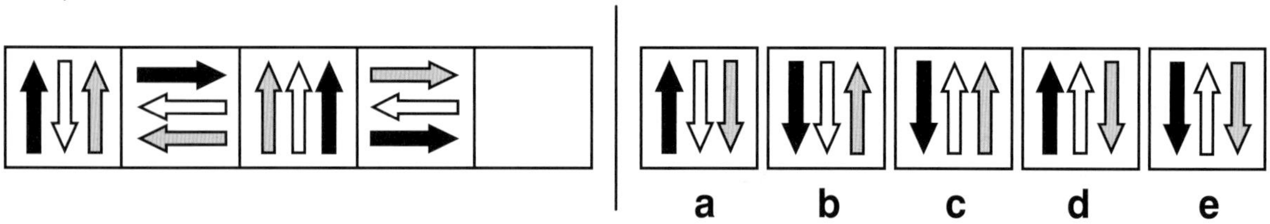

8)

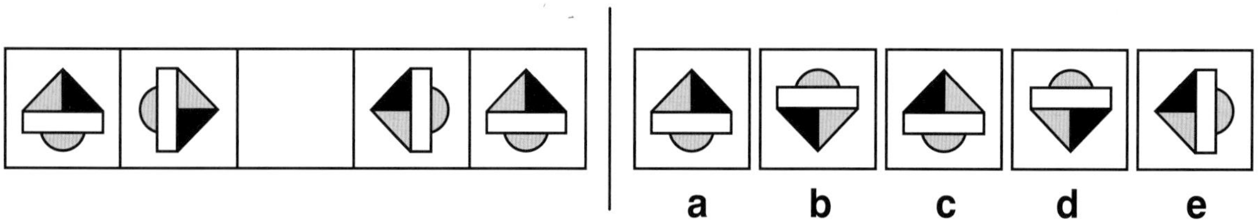

9)

10)

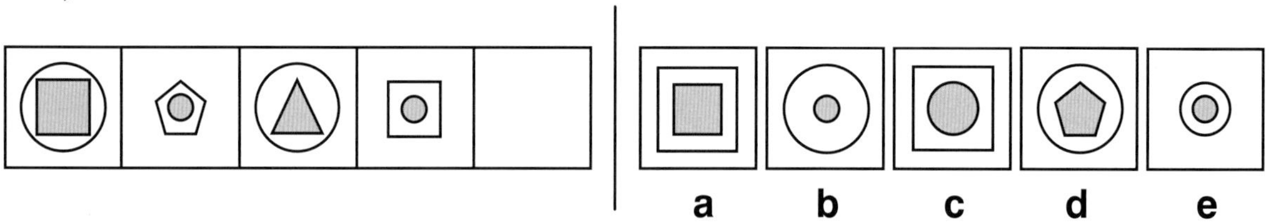

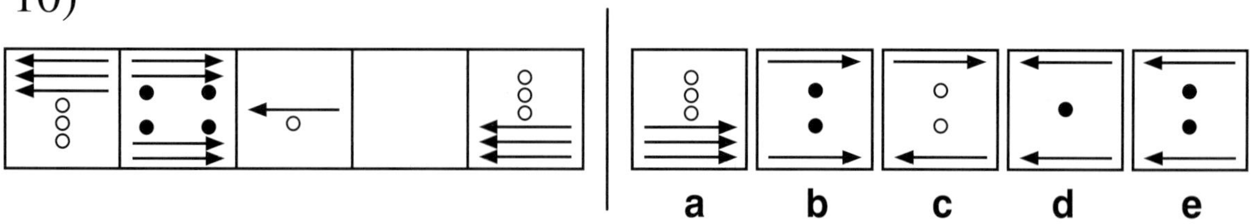

Score

Section D

The following figures correspond to the codes next to them. You must decide how the code letters go with the figures and then find the correct code for the Test Figure.

Example

● AZ

■ BZ

▲ CY

TEST FIGURE

CZ	BY	AY	BZ	AZ
a	b	ⓒ	d	e

Now do the questions below. Circle the correct answer.

1)

XT

XU

ZV

TEST FIGURE

ZU	XT	XU	ZT	XV
a	b	c	d	e

2)

BHV

BGW

AGV

TEST FIGURE

BGV	AHW	AHV	AGV	BHW
a	b	c	d	e

3)

CMT

ENS

DOT

AMS

TEST FIGURE

CNS	EOS	CMS	ENT	DMS
a	b	c	d	e

4)

⬤ (circle with black dot)	AZT
▢ (square with open circle)	BZS
⬡ (hexagon with black square)	CYT

TEST FIGURE: hexagon with open square

AYS	BYS	CYS	CZS	AZT
a	b	c	d	e

5)

shaded circle with horizontal line	PH
circle with horizontal line	QH
shaded square with horizontal line	RG

TEST FIGURE: square with horizontal line

QH	PG	PH	RG	QG
a	b	c	d	e

6)

dotted square with open circle	XHT
circle with black square	WFS
square with shaded square	YHS
dashed triangle with black circle	WGT

TEST FIGURE: dashed triangle with open square

YGT	XGT	WHS	YGS	XFS
a	b	c	d	e

7)

triangle with shaded segment	PDJ
rectangle split horizontally	RCK
circle with horizontal lines	PEM
shaded pentagon	RDL

TEST FIGURE: rectangle with vertical lines

PDK	REJ	PDM	PEK	RCM
a	b	c	d	e

8)

rounded rectangle with black up-triangle	CWG
rounded rectangle with shaded down-triangle	BXH
rounded rectangle with left-triangle	AWJ
rounded rectangle with black right-triangle	DXG

TEST FIGURE: rounded rectangle with open down-triangle

AXG	BWH	DXJ	CWJ	BWJ
a	b	c	d	e

Score ▢

Non-verbal Reasoning Test 7
Section A

The following figures correspond to the codes next to them. You must decide how the code letters go with the figures and then find the correct code for the Test Figure.

Example

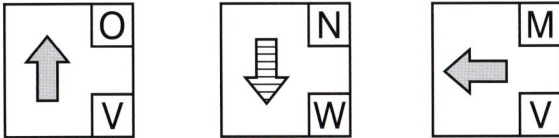

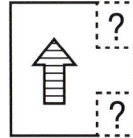

TEST FIGURE

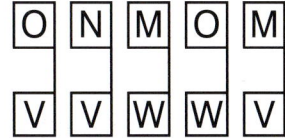

a b c (d) e

Now do the questions below. Circle the correct answer.

1)

TEST FIGURE

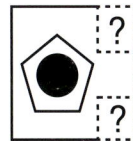

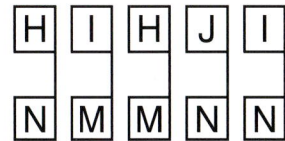

a b c d e

2)

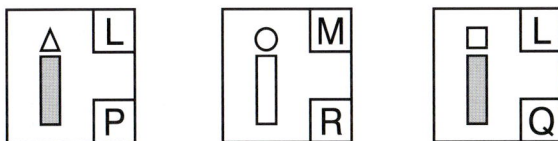

TEST FIGURE

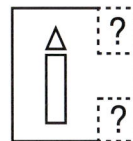

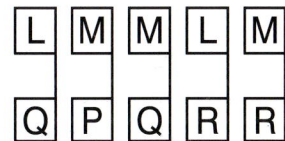

a b c d e

3)

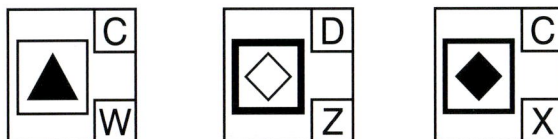

TEST FIGURE

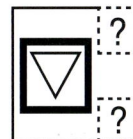

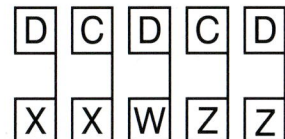

a b c d e

4)

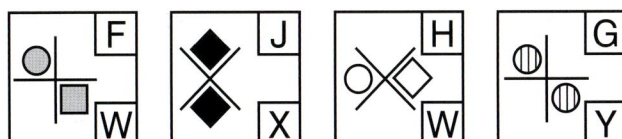

TEST FIGURE

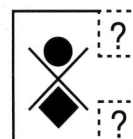

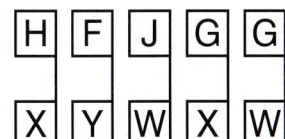

a b c d e

5)

TEST FIGURE

	A	D	D	C	C
	M	L	N	M	N
	a	b	c	d	e

6)

TEST FIGURE

	O	R	P	R	O
	K	K	J	L	J
	a	b	c	d	e

7)

TEST FIGURE

	B	C	D	B	D
	X	X	Y	Z	W
	a	b	c	d	e

8)

TEST FIGURE

	C	B	C	D	A
	U	U	V	V	T
	a	b	c	d	e

9)

TEST FIGURE

	D	C	D	A	C
	T	S	R	T	R
	a	b	c	d	e

Score

Section B

On the left of each row are two shapes with an arrow between them. Decide how the second shape is related to the first. After these there is a third shape, then an arrow and then five more shapes. Decide which of the five shapes goes with the third shape to make a pair like the two shapes on the left.

Example

a   b   c   (d)   e

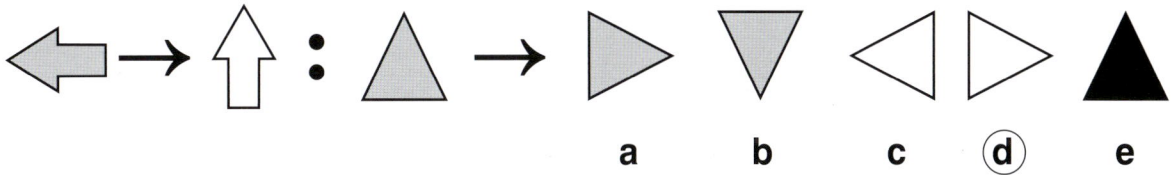

Now do the questions below. Circle the correct answer.

1)

a   b   c   d   e

2)

a   b   c   d   e

3)

a   b   c   d   e

4)

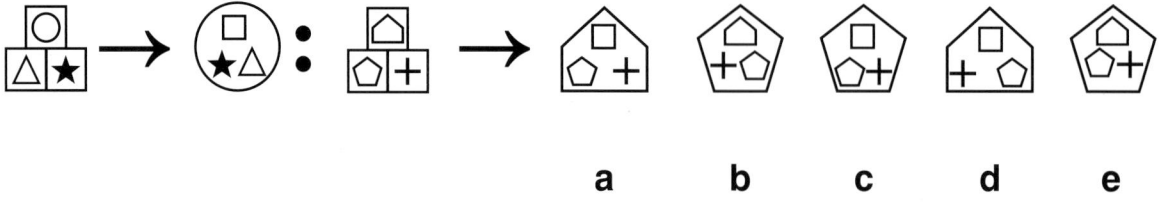

                      a   **b**   **c**   **d**   **e**

5)

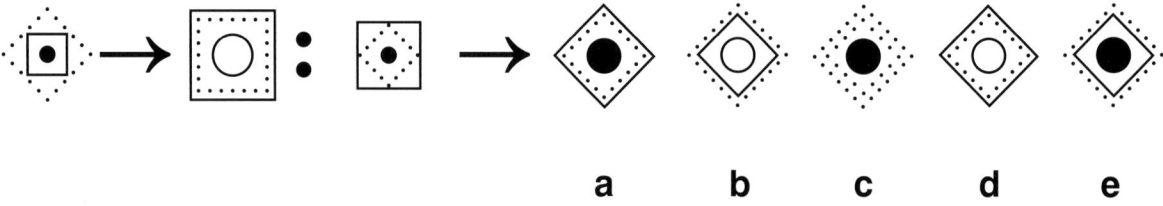

                      a   **b**   **c**   **d**   **e**

6)

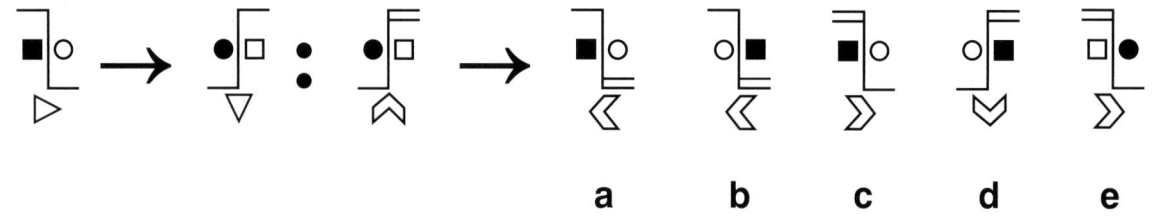

                      a   **b**   **c**   **d**   **e**

7)

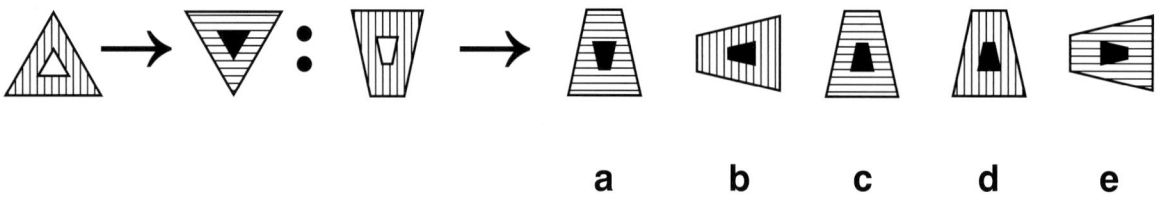

                      a   **b**   **c**   **d**   **e**

8)

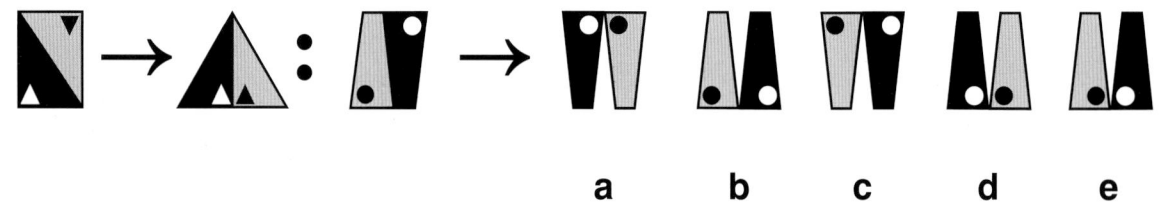

                      a   **b**   **c**   **d**   **e**

Score

Section C

In the big square on the left of each line below, one of the small squares has been left empty. One of the five figures on the right should fill the empty square. Find this figure.

Example

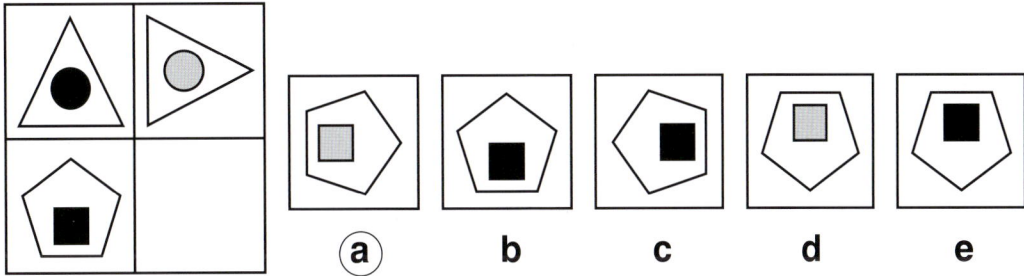

Now do the questions below. Circle the correct answer.

1)

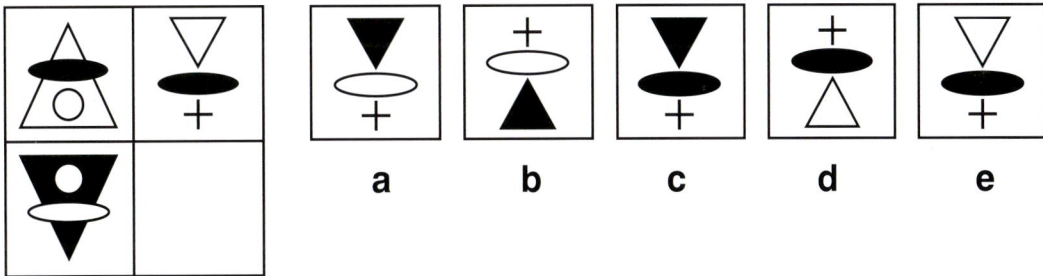

2)

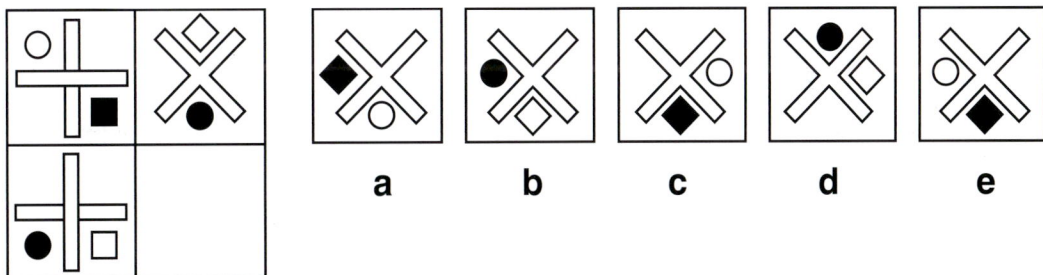

3)

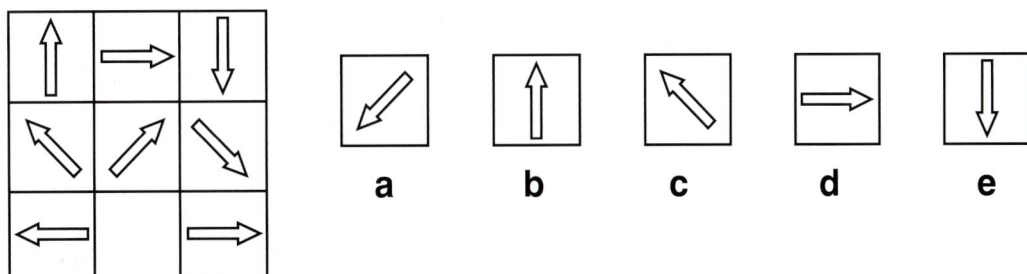

4)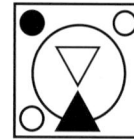

a   **b**   **c**   **d**   **e**

5)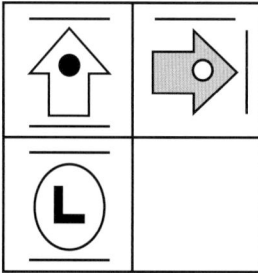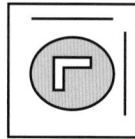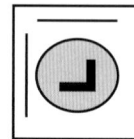

a   **b**   **c**   **d**   **e**

6)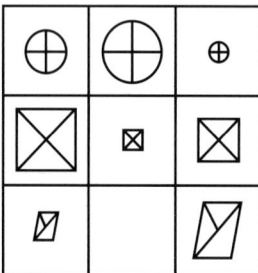

a   **b**   **c**   **d**   **e**

7)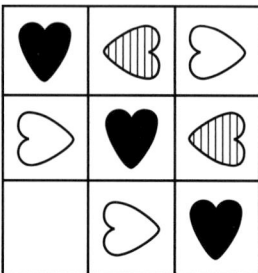

a   **b**   **c**   **d**   **e**

8)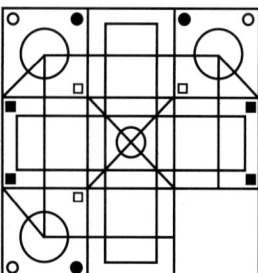

a   **b**   **c**   **d**   **e**

Score

Section D

On the left of each of the rows below there are two figures that are alike. On the right there are five more figures. Find which one of these five is **most like** the two figures on the left.

Example

| a | b | c | d | e |

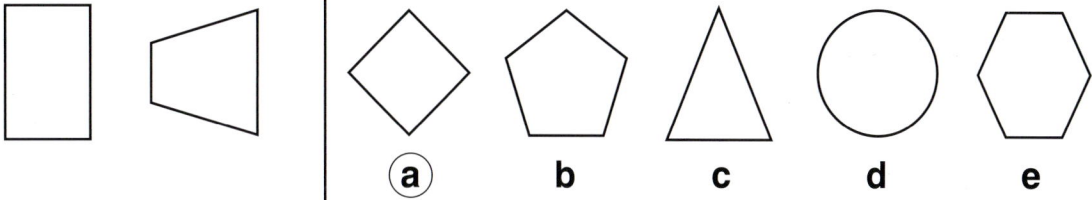

Now do the questions below. Circle the correct answer.

1)

| a | b | c | d | e |

2)

| a | b | c | d | e |

3)

| a | b | c | d | e |

4)

| a | b | c | d | e |

5)

a   b   c   d   e

6)

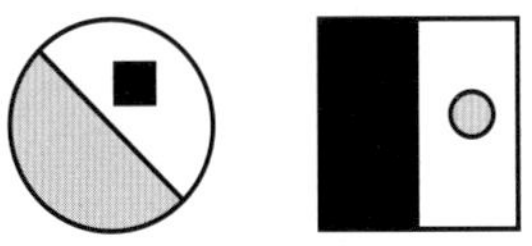

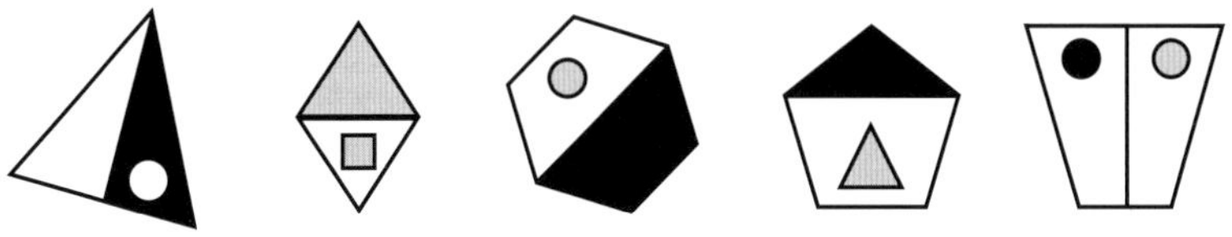

a   b   c   d   e

7)

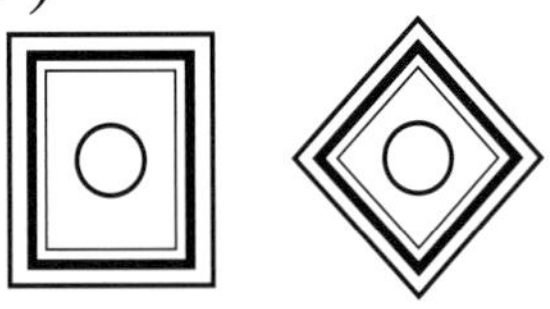

a   b   c   d   e

8)

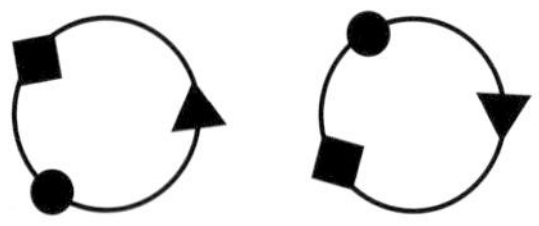

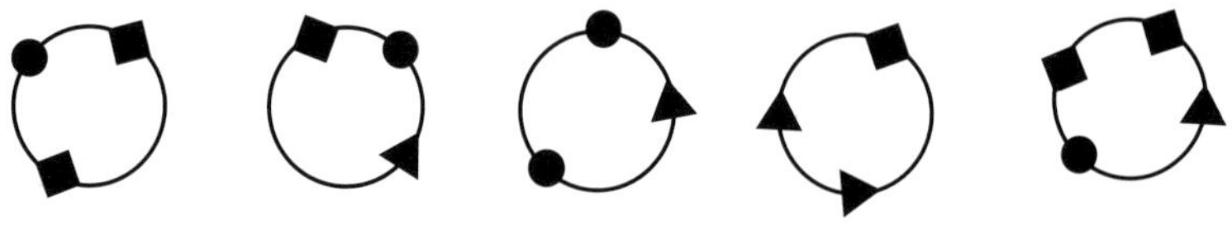

a   b   c   d   e

9)

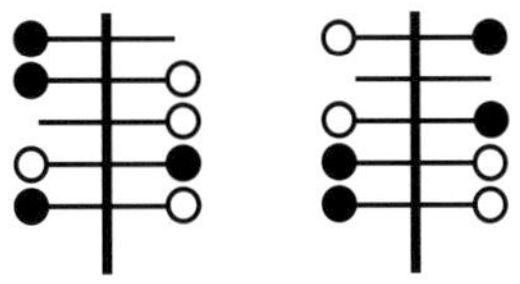

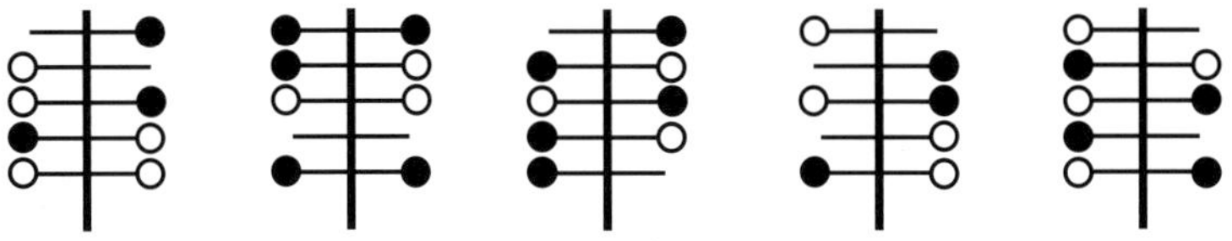

a   b   c   d   e

10)

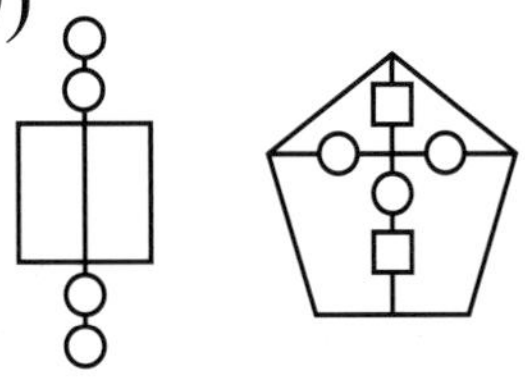

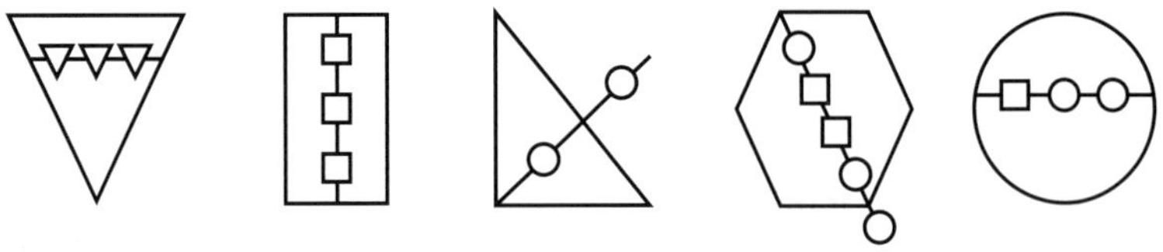

a   b   c   d   e

Score [ ]

Non-verbal Reasoning Test 8
Section A

On the left of each of the rows below there are two figures that are alike. On the right there are five more figures. Find which one of these five is **most like** the two figures on the left.

Example

a b c d e

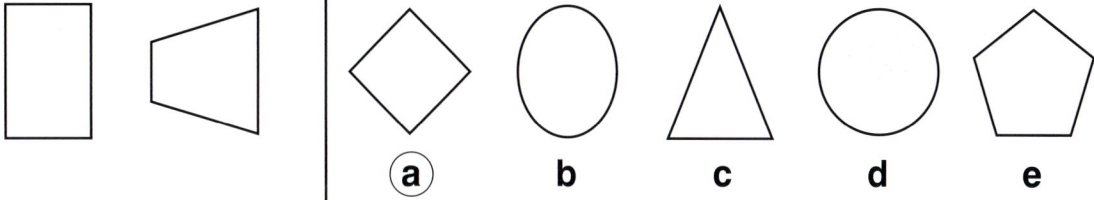

Now do the questions below. Circle the correct answer.

1)

a b c d e

2)

a b c d e

3)

a b c d e

4)

a b c d e

5)

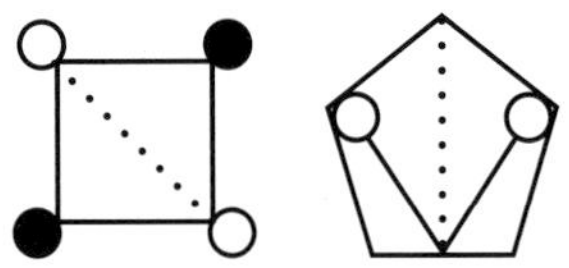

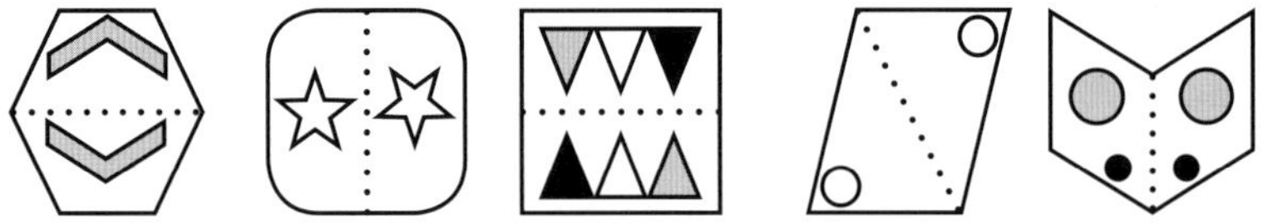

a   b   c   d   e

6)

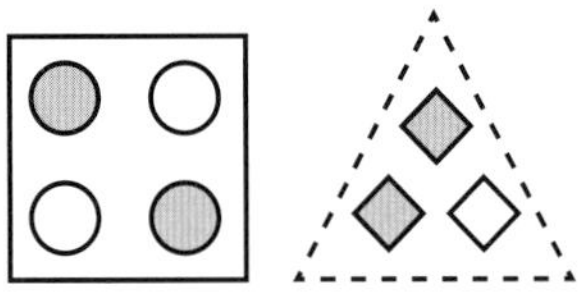

a   b   c   d   e

7)

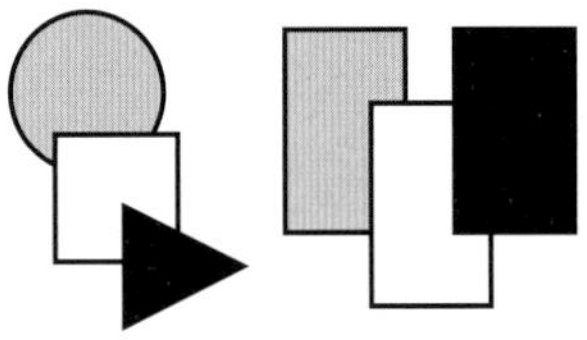

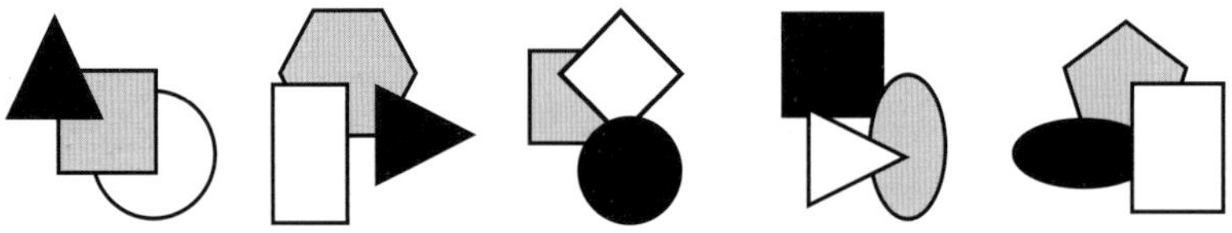

a   b   c   d   e

8)

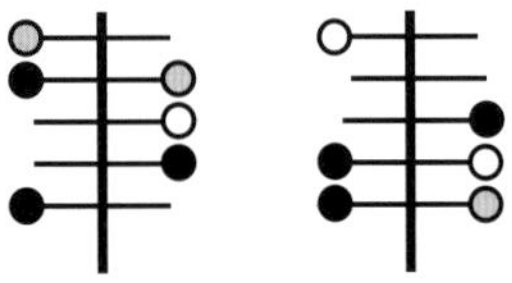

a   b   c   d   e

9)

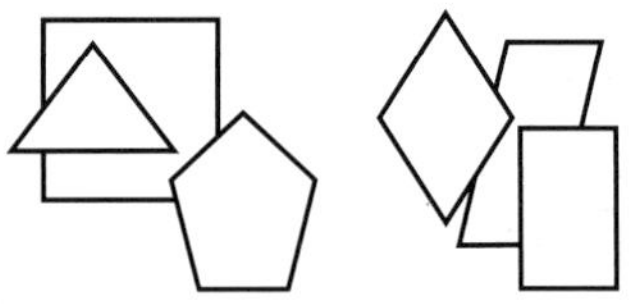

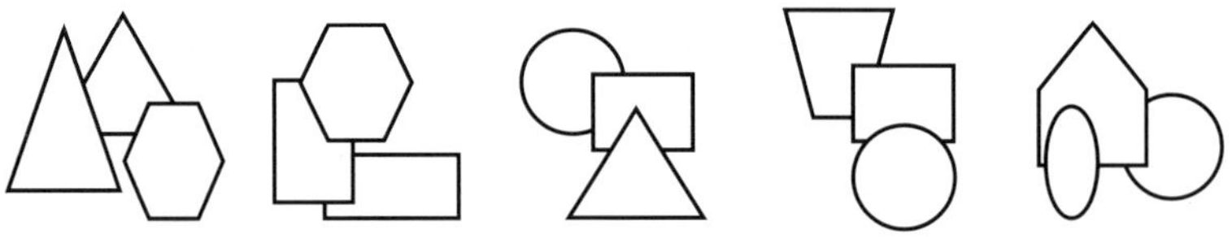

a   b   c   d   e

Score

Section B

To the left of each of the lines below there are five squares arranged in order. One of these squares has been left empty. Find which one of the five squares on the right should take the place of the empty square.

Example

Now do the questions below. Circle the correct answer.

1)

2)

3)

4)

5)

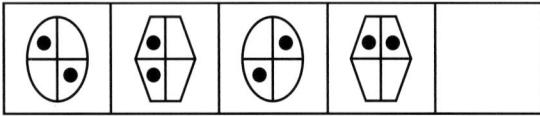 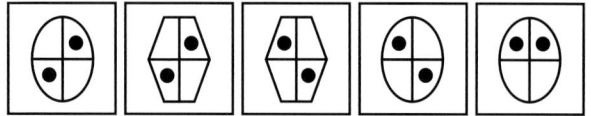

a   b   c   d   e

6)

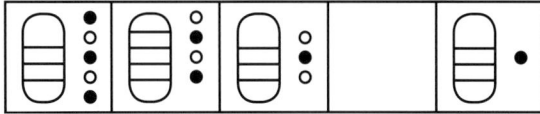 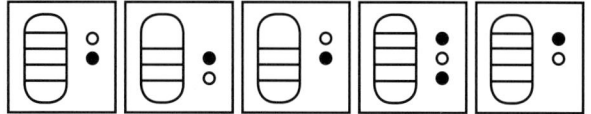

a   b   c   d   e

7)

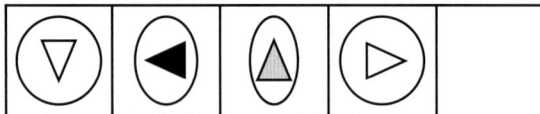 

a   b   c   d   e

8)

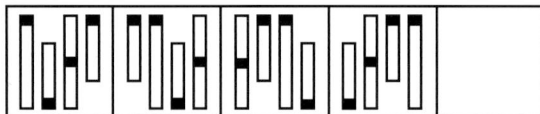 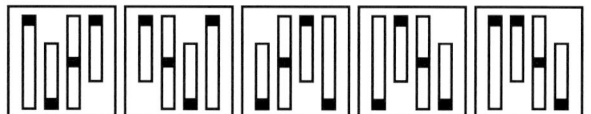

a   b   c   d   e

9)

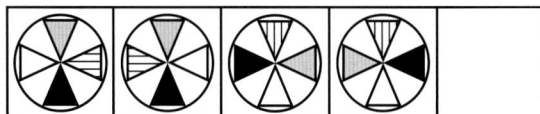 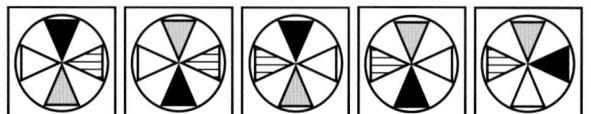

a   b   c   d   e

10)

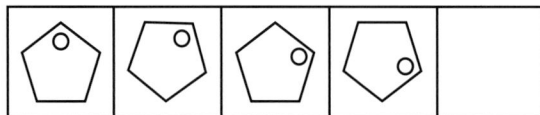 

a   b   c   d   e

Score

Section C

In each of the rows below there are five figures. Find one figure in each row that is **most unlike** the other four.

Example

 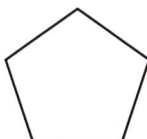 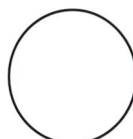 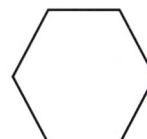

| a | b | c | (d) | e |

Now do the questions below. Circle the correct answer.

1)

 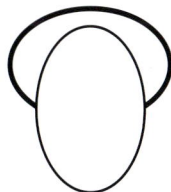 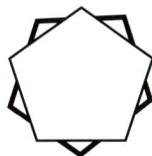  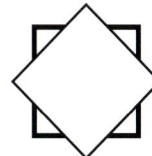

| a | b | c | d | e |

2)

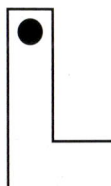 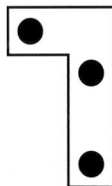  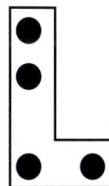 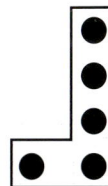

| a | b | c | d | e |

3)

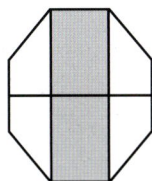 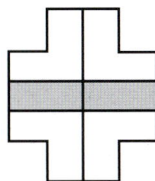 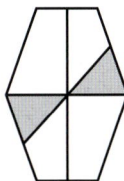 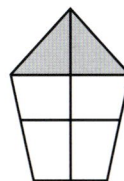 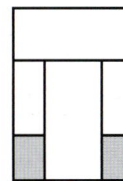

| a | b | c | d | e |

4)

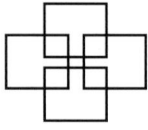  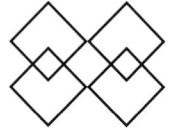

a **b** **c** **d** **e**

5)

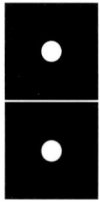 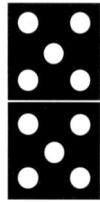  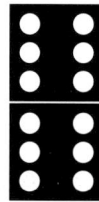 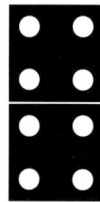

a **b** **c** **d** **e**

6)

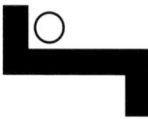    

a **b** **c** **d** **e**

7)

a **b** **c** **d** **e**

8)

   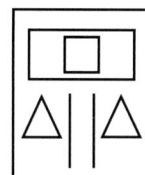 

a **b** **c** **d** **e**

Score

Section D

The following figures correspond to the codes next to them. You must decide how the code letters go with the figures and then find the correct code for the Test Figure.

Example

●	AZ
■	BZ
▲	CY

TEST FIGURE	CZ	BY	AY	BZ	AZ
◯	a	b	(c)	d	e

Now do the questions below. Circle the correct answer.

1)

(house shape, grey)	DRM
(house shape, white)	DTN
(arrow shape, lined)	ESM

TEST FIGURE	ETM	DSM	DRN	ERN	DSN
(grey arrow)	a	b	c	d	e

2)

(pentagon with oval)	PD
(pentagon with plus)	QE
(pentagon with circle)	QF

TEST FIGURE	PE	QE	QD	PF	PD
(pentagon with small circle)	a	b	c	d	e

3)

(oval with two triangles)	TEM
(oval with two circles)	TFN
(square with triangle)	SEO
(rectangle with filled and open circle)	SFM

TEST FIGURE	SFN	TFO	TEN	SEN	TEO
(oval with two triangles pointing right)	a	b	c	d	e

4)

GL

FM

EL

TEST FIGURE

EL	FL	EM	GM	GL
a	**b**	**c**	**d**	**e**

5)

EP

FO

FQ

TEST FIGURE

EQ	FP	FO	EO	EP
a	**b**	**c**	**d**	**e**

6)

AJW

DHX

AGY

BFW

TEST FIGURE

DJW	BJX	AHW	DFY	BGY
a	**b**	**c**	**d**	**e**

7)

BRH

ATF

BSG

AQG

TEST FIGURE

ASF	BQG	BTG	ARG	BSF
a	**b**	**c**	**d**	**e**

8)

TWB

RXC

SWD

TXC

TEST FIGURE

TXD	SXB	TWC	SXD	RWC
a	**b**	**c**	**d**	**e**

Score

Multiple-choice Answer Sheet
11+ Non-verbal Reasoning Year 5-7 Testbook 2
Test 1

Section A

EXAMPLE
- a
- b ▬
- c
- d
- e

1	2	3	4	5
a b c d e	a b c d e	a b c d e	a b c d e	a b c d e

6	7	8	9
a b c d e	a b c d e	a b c d e	a b c d e

Section B

EXAMPLE
- a ▬
- b
- c
- d
- e

1	2	3	4	5
a b c d e	a b c d e	a b c d e	a b c d e	a b c d e

6	7	8
a b c d e	a b c d e	a b c d e

Section C

EXAMPLE
- a
- b
- c
- d ▬
- e

1	2	3	4	5
a b c d e	a b c d e	a b c d e	a b c d e	a b c d e

6	7	8
a b c d e	a b c d e	a b c d e

Section D

EXAMPLE
- a
- b
- c
- d ▬
- e

1	2	3	4	5
a b c d e	a b c d e	a b c d e	a b c d e	a b c d e

6	7	8	9	10
a b c d e	a b c d e	a b c d e	a b c d e	a b c d e

Multiple-choice Answer Sheet
11+ Non-verbal Reasoning Year 5-7 Testbook 2
Test 2

Section A

EXAMPLE	1	2	3	4	5
a ▭ b ▭ c ▭ d ▬ e ▭	a ▭ b ▭ c ▭ d ▭ e ▭	a ▭ b ▭ c ▭ d ▭ e ▭	a ▭ b ▭ c ▭ d ▭ e ▭	a ▭ b ▭ c ▭ d ▭ e ▭	a ▭ b ▭ c ▭ d ▭ e ▭

6	7	8
a ▭ b ▭ c ▭ d ▭ e ▭	a ▭ b ▭ c ▭ d ▭ e ▭	a ▭ b ▭ c ▭ d ▭ e ▭

Section B

EXAMPLE	1	2	3	4	5
a ▭ b ▭ c ▭ d ▬ e ▭	a ▭ b ▭ c ▭ d ▭ e ▭	a ▭ b ▭ c ▭ d ▭ e ▭	a ▭ b ▭ c ▭ d ▭ e ▭	a ▭ b ▭ c ▭ d ▭ e ▭	a ▭ b ▭ c ▭ d ▭ e ▭

6	7	8	9
a ▭ b ▭ c ▭ d ▭ e ▭	a ▭ b ▭ c ▭ d ▭ e ▭	a ▭ b ▭ c ▭ d ▭ e ▭	a ▭ b ▭ c ▭ d ▭ e ▭

Section C

EXAMPLE	1	2	3	4	5
a ▭ b ▭ c ▬ d ▭ e ▭	a ▭ b ▭ c ▭ d ▭ e ▭	a ▭ b ▭ c ▭ d ▭ e ▭	a ▭ b ▭ c ▭ d ▭ e ▭	a ▭ b ▭ c ▭ d ▭ e ▭	a ▭ b ▭ c ▭ d ▭ e ▭

6	7	8
a ▭ b ▭ c ▭ d ▭ e ▭	a ▭ b ▭ c ▭ d ▭ e ▭	a ▭ b ▭ c ▭ d ▭ e ▭

Section D

EXAMPLE	1	2	3	4	5
a ▬ b ▭ c ▭ d ▭ e ▭	a ▭ b ▭ c ▭ d ▭ e ▭	a ▭ b ▭ c ▭ d ▭ e ▭	a ▭ b ▭ c ▭ d ▭ e ▭	a ▭ b ▭ c ▭ d ▭ e ▭	a ▭ b ▭ c ▭ d ▭ e ▭

6	7	8	9	10
a ▭ b ▭ c ▭ d ▭ e ▭	a ▭ b ▭ c ▭ d ▭ e ▭	a ▭ b ▭ c ▭ d ▭ e ▭	a ▭ b ▭ c ▭ d ▭ e ▭	a ▭ b ▭ c ▭ d ▭ e ▭

Multiple-choice Answer Sheet
11+ Non-verbal Reasoning Year 5-7 Testbook 2
Test 3

Section A

EXAMPLE: a, b, c, d ▬, e

1	2	3	4	5
a b c d e	a b c d e	a b c d e	a b c d e	a b c d e

6	7	8	9
a b c d e	a b c d e	a b c d e	a b c d e

Section B

EXAMPLE: a ▬, b, c, d, e

1	2	3	4	5
a b c d e	a b c d e	a b c d e	a b c d e	a b c d e

6	7	8
a b c d e	a b c d e	a b c d e

Section C

EXAMPLE: a, b ▬, c, d, e

1	2	3	4	5
a b c d e	a b c d e	a b c d e	a b c d e	a b c d e

6	7	8	9	10
a b c d e	a b c d e	a b c d e	a b c d e	a b c d e

Section D

EXAMPLE: a, b, c, d ▬, e

1	2	3	4	5
a b c d e	a b c d e	a b c d e	a b c d e	a b c d e

6	7	8
a b c d e	a b c d e	a b c d e

Section A

EXAMPLE: a, b, c, d (filled), e

1: a, b, c, d, e
2: a, b, c, d, e
3: a, b, c, d, e
4: a, b, c, d, e
5: a, b, c, d, e
6: a, b, c, d, e
7: a, b, c, d, e
8: a, b, c, d, e
9: a, b, c, d, e

Section B

EXAMPLE: a (filled), b, c, d, e

1: a, b, c, d, e
2: a, b, c, d, e
3: a, b, c, d, e
4: a, b, c, d, e
5: a, b, c, d, e
6: a, b, c, d, e
7: a, b, c, d, e
8: a, b, c, d, e

Section C

EXAMPLE: a, b, c (filled), d, e

1: a, b, c, d, e
2: a, b, c, d, e
3: a, b, c, d, e
4: a, b, c, d, e
5: a, b, c, d, e
6: a, b, c, d, e
7: a, b, c, d, e
8: a, b, c, d, e

Section D

EXAMPLE: a (filled), b, c, d, e

1: a, b, c, d, e
2: a, b, c, d, e
3: a, b, c, d, e
4: a, b, c, d, e
5: a, b, c, d, e
6: a, b, c, d, e
7: a, b, c, d, e
8: a, b, c, d, e
9: a, b, c, d, e
10: a, b, c, d, e

Multiple-choice Answer Sheet
11+ Non-verbal Reasoning Year 5-7 Testbook 2
Test 5

Section A

EXAMPLE: a, b (marked), c, d, e

1, 2, 3, 4, 5, 6, 7, 8, 9 — each with options a, b, c, d, e

Section B

EXAMPLE: a, b, c, d (marked), e

1, 2, 3, 4, 5, 6, 7, 8 — each with options a, b, c, d, e

Section C

EXAMPLE: a, b, c, d (marked), e

1, 2, 3, 4, 5, 6, 7, 8 — each with options a, b, c, d, e

Section D

EXAMPLE: a, b, c, d (marked), e

1, 2, 3, 4, 5, 6, 7, 8, 9, 10 — each with options a, b, c, d, e

Multiple-choice Answer Sheet
11+ Non-verbal Reasoning Year 5-7 Testbook 2
Test 6

Section A

EXAMPLE
a ▬
b ▭
c ▭
d ▭
e ▭

1 a ▭ b ▭ c ▭ d ▭ e ▭

2 a ▭ b ▭ c ▭ d ▭ e ▭

3 a ▭ b ▭ c ▭ d ▭ e ▭

4 a ▭ b ▭ c ▭ d ▭ e ▭

5 a ▭ b ▭ c ▭ d ▭ e ▭

6 a ▭ b ▭ c ▭ d ▭ e ▭

7 a ▭ b ▭ c ▭ d ▭ e ▭

8 a ▭ b ▭ c ▭ d ▭ e ▭

9 a ▭ b ▭ c ▭ d ▭ e ▭

Section B

EXAMPLE
a ▬
b ▭
c ▭
d ▭
e ▭

1 a ▭ b ▭ c ▭ d ▭ e ▭

2 a ▭ b ▭ c ▭ d ▭ e ▭

3 a ▭ b ▭ c ▭ d ▭ e ▭

4 a ▭ b ▭ c ▭ d ▭ e ▭

5 a ▭ b ▭ c ▭ d ▭ e ▭

6 a ▭ b ▭ c ▭ d ▭ e ▭

7 a ▭ b ▭ c ▭ d ▭ e ▭

8 a ▭ b ▭ c ▭ d ▭ e ▭

Section C

EXAMPLE
a ▭
b ▬
c ▭
d ▭
e ▭

1 a ▭ b ▭ c ▭ d ▭ e ▭

2 a ▭ b ▭ c ▭ d ▭ e ▭

3 a ▭ b ▭ c ▭ d ▭ e ▭

4 a ▭ b ▭ c ▭ d ▭ e ▭

5 a ▭ b ▭ c ▭ d ▭ e ▭

6 a ▭ b ▭ c ▭ d ▭ e ▭

7 a ▭ b ▭ c ▭ d ▭ e ▭

8 a ▭ b ▭ c ▭ d ▭ e ▭

9 a ▭ b ▭ c ▭ d ▭ e ▭

10 a ▭ b ▭ c ▭ d ▭ e ▭

Section D

EXAMPLE
a ▭
b ▭
c ▬
d ▭
e ▭

1 a ▭ b ▭ c ▭ d ▭ e ▭

2 a ▭ b ▭ c ▭ d ▭ e ▭

3 a ▭ b ▭ c ▭ d ▭ e ▭

4 a ▭ b ▭ c ▭ d ▭ e ▭

5 a ▭ b ▭ c ▭ d ▭ e ▭

6 a ▭ b ▭ c ▭ d ▭ e ▭

7 a ▭ b ▭ c ▭ d ▭ e ▭

8 a ▭ b ▭ c ▭ d ▭ e ▭

Multiple-choice Answer Sheet
11+ Non-verbal Reasoning Year 5-7 Testbook 2
Test 7

Section A

EXAMPLE
a
b
c
d
e

1	2	3	4	5
a b c d e	a b c d e	a b c d e	a b c d e	a b c d e

6	7	8	9
a b c d e	a b c d e	a b c d e	a b c d e

Section B

EXAMPLE
a
b
c
d
e

1	2	3	4	5
a b c d e	a b c d e	a b c d e	a b c d e	a b c d e

6	7	8
a b c d e	a b c d e	a b c d e

Section C

EXAMPLE
a
b
c
d
e

1	2	3	4	5
a b c d e	a b c d e	a b c d e	a b c d e	a b c d e

6	7	8
a b c d e	a b c d e	a b c d e

Section D

EXAMPLE
a
b
c
d
e

1	2	3	4	5
a b c d e	a b c d e	a b c d e	a b c d e	a b c d e

6	7	8	9	10
a b c d e	a b c d e	a b c d e	a b c d e	a b c d e

Multiple-choice Answer Sheet
11+ Non-verbal Reasoning Year 5-7 Testbook 2
Test 8

Section A

EXAMPLE: a ▄ b ☐ c ☐ d ☐ e ☐

1: a ☐ b ☐ c ☐ d ☐ e ☐
2: a ☐ b ☐ c ☐ d ☐ e ☐
3: a ☐ b ☐ c ☐ d ☐ e ☐
4: a ☐ b ☐ c ☐ d ☐ e ☐
5: a ☐ b ☐ c ☐ d ☐ e ☐

6: a ☐ b ☐ c ☐ d ☐ e ☐
7: a ☐ b ☐ c ☐ d ☐ e ☐
8: a ☐ b ☐ c ☐ d ☐ e ☐
9: a ☐ b ☐ c ☐ d ☐ e ☐

Section B

EXAMPLE: a ☐ b ▄ c ☐ d ☐ e ☐

1: a ☐ b ☐ c ☐ d ☐ e ☐
2: a ☐ b ☐ c ☐ d ☐ e ☐
3: a ☐ b ☐ c ☐ d ☐ e ☐
4: a ☐ b ☐ c ☐ d ☐ e ☐
5: a ☐ b ☐ c ☐ d ☐ e ☐

6: a ☐ b ☐ c ☐ d ☐ e ☐
7: a ☐ b ☐ c ☐ d ☐ e ☐
8: a ☐ b ☐ c ☐ d ☐ e ☐
9: a ☐ b ☐ c ☐ d ☐ e ☐
10: a ☐ b ☐ c ☐ d ☐ e ☐

Section C

EXAMPLE: a ☐ b ☐ c ☐ d ▄ e ☐

1: a ☐ b ☐ c ☐ d ☐ e ☐
2: a ☐ b ☐ c ☐ d ☐ e ☐
3: a ☐ b ☐ c ☐ d ☐ e ☐
4: a ☐ b ☐ c ☐ d ☐ e ☐
5: a ☐ b ☐ c ☐ d ☐ e ☐

6: a ☐ b ☐ c ☐ d ☐ e ☐
7: a ☐ b ☐ c ☐ d ☐ e ☐
8: a ☐ b ☐ c ☐ d ☐ e ☐

Section D

EXAMPLE: a ☐ b ☐ c ▄ d ☐ e ☐

1: a ☐ b ☐ c ☐ d ☐ e ☐
2: a ☐ b ☐ c ☐ d ☐ e ☐
3: a ☐ b ☐ c ☐ d ☐ e ☐
4: a ☐ b ☐ c ☐ d ☐ e ☐
5: a ☐ b ☐ c ☐ d ☐ e ☐

6: a ☐ b ☐ c ☐ d ☐ e ☐
7: a ☐ b ☐ c ☐ d ☐ e ☐
8: a ☐ b ☐ c ☐ d ☐ e ☐

Answers

Non-verbal Reasoning Test 1
Section A

Example - b - The figure rotates 90° clockwise. One Arrow is subtracted.

1) **b** - The Ellipse squashes then stretches. The Triangle rotates 90° clockwise. The order of fills is: Grey, Black, White, Grey, Black.

2) **a** - The figure flips vertically. The number of Lines alternates between one and two. The order of enclosed shapes is: Square, Circle, Triangle, Square, Circle.

3) **b** - One Circle moves from the centre into the next corner anticlockwise.

4) **c** - The figure rotates 90° clockwise. The Black and White Fills alternate.

5) **d** - The Thin and Thick Outlines swap. The order of fills is: Black, White, Grey, Black, White.

6) **b** - The figure rotates 45° clockwise. The enclosed Circle moves up one position. The Black and White Fills swap.

7) **c** - The order of fills of the Circle is: Black, White, Grey, Black, White. The shape alternates between a 5-sided shape and a 6-sided shape. The shape with a White Fill rotates 90° clockwise. The Line vertically transposes.

8) **a** - The number of Circles is: 2, 3, 4, 3, 2. The number of Lines is: 3, 2, 1, 2, 3.

9) **b** - The Triangles on the outer Circle point clockwise. The Triangles on the inner Circle point anticlockwise. The order of fills of the enclosed Circle is: Black, Grey, Lined, Black, Grey.

Section B

Example - a - Solved horizontally: The figure has been rotated 90° clockwise. The Black Fill has become Grey.

1) **c** - Solved vertically: The figure has been reflected across the horizontal mid-line of the matrix. The Grey Fill has become Black.

2) **d** - Solved vertically: The figure has been reflected across the horizontal mid-line of the matrix. The White Fill has become Grey. The Thick Line Types have become Thin.

3) **b** - Solved horizontally: The Triangle has been rotated 90° clockwise. There must be one Triangle with a Grey Fill and two Triangles with the same Lined Fill.

4) **e** - Solved vertically: The original top right shape has become the new outer shape with a Thick Outline. The original bottom right shape has become the new left enclosed shape. The original left shape has become the new right enclosed shape.

5) **c** - Solved horizontally: The figure has been flipped vertically. The Vertical Line has become Solid.

6) **c** - Solved vertically: The Lines have been rotated 90° anticlockwise. The Black and White Fills have been alternated.

7) **c** - Solved horizontally: There must be two small shapes and one large shape. There must be one Triangle, one Square and one Pentagon. There must be two shapes with a Black Fill and one shape with a White Fill.

8) **d** - Solved vertically: The figure has been rotated 90° clockwise. The fills have been alternated.

Section C

Example - d - The figure is not Straight-edged.

1) **e** - The Lined Fill is not Horizontal Lined.

2) **b** - The enclosed shape is not the same as the outer shape.

3) **d** - There is not the same number of each fill.

4) **e** - There is not an even number of Circles.

5) **d** - There is not one more Line than Arrows.

6) **d** - The large shape does not overlay one of the smaller shapes.

Answers

7) **a** - The figure is an inversion of the others, not a rotation.

8) **c** - There is not the same number of each fill.

Section D

Example - **d** - O - Arrow points upwards; W - Horizontal Lined Fill

1) **a** - D - Figures are in the middle of the square; X - Two Heart Shapes have a Grey Fill

2) **e** - K - Circle; G - Three Horizontal Lines

3) **a** - D - White Fill; Z - Thick Outline

4) **e** - E - Horizontal figure; P - Circles

5) **d** - E - Shape in top right corner of the square; R - Square

6) **b** - N - Four shapes; E - Circles

7) **d** - D - One shape; S - White Fill

8) **e** - X - Three Lines; T - White Fill

9) **a** - F - Figure is on the left of the square; T - Two Black Fills

10) **d** - T - Horizontal Line is at the bottom of the square; C - Two White Fills

Non-verbal Reasoning Test 2
Section A

Example - **d** - The figure rotates 90° clockwise. The fill becomes White.

1) **e** - The figure rotates 90° clockwise. The enclosed shape vertically transposes and the fill becomes White.

2) **d** - The shapes swap positions.

3) **b** - The figure rotates 90° clockwise. The smaller shape with a White Fill rotates a further 180°.

4) **d** - The figure rotates 90° clockwise. The left enclosed letter rotates a further 90° anticlockwise. The right enclosed letter rotates a further 90° clockwise.

5) **b** - The figure flips vertically.

6) **b** - The figure rotates 180°. The enclosed shape rotates a further 90°.

7) **e** - The figure rotates 180°. The Grey Fill becomes Black and the Black Fill becomes White. The enclosed Square becomes a Circle.

8) **b** - The top and bottom figures swap. The Black and White Fills swap.

Section B

Example - **d** - The figure is not Straight-edged.

1) **e** - The enclosed Line is not a rotation of the other figures.

2) **a** - The figure does not have four sides.

3) **c** - One of the small shapes does not join to the large shape by a side.

4) **c** - The figure does not have two enclosed Lines.

5) **d** - There is not four of one line ending and two of the other.

6) **b** - There are not three shapes with a White Fill.

7) **e** - The corners of the enclosed shape do not touch the Circle.

8) **a** - The figure does not contain a Triangle.

9) **a** - The enclosed shapes are not the same.

Section C

Example - **c** - A - Circle; Y - Grey Fill

1) **e** - A - Pentagon points downwards; R - Circle has a White Fill

2) **b** - G - House Shape points upwards; C - Enclosed shape is a Circle

3) **b** - K - Two Arrows have a Black Fill; D - Arrows point to the left

4) **a** - W - Figure points downwards; D - Triangle has a Black Fill; R - Enclosed Circle

5) **c** - M - Cross has a Grey Fill; G - Cross is horizontal

6) **a** - K - Small Circle has a Grey Fill; G - Small figure; C - Large shape is a Circle

7) **a** - V - Two Squares; C - Vertical Lined Fill

8) **a** - E - Arrow points to the right; J - Left Slant Lined Fill

Answers

Section D

Example - **a** - The shape has four sides.

1) **e** - The Triangle has a right angle.

2) **d** - The figure has two linked identical shapes with Grey and White Fills.

3) **d** - The linkage has four sides.

4) **c** - The figure has three White Fills, two Grey Fills and one Black Fill.

5) **c** - The figure consists of three Circles, two Lines and one Rectangle with a Dashed Outline.

6) **a** - The large shape overlays one small shape, and one small shape overlays the large shape. There is one enclosure.

7) **e** - There are two identical shapes perpendicular to each other that are merged.

8) **e** - The number of small shapes is equal to the number of sides of the large shape.

9) **d** - The shape at the base of the flag and the shape enclosed in the flag have Black and Grey Fills. The flag points to the left. The number of sides of the outer shape of the flag and the base shape totals eight.

10) **e** - There are two enclosed Lines. The figure is a rotation of the Test Figures.

Non-verbal Reasoning Test 3
Section A

Example - **d** - O - Arrow points upwards; W - Horizontal Lined Fill

1) **a** - E - Ellipse has a White Fill; Z - Pentagon

2) **e** - A - Circle has a White Fill; R - Figure faces left

3) **d** - H - Four short Lines; B - Lines are at the bottom of the figure

4) **a** - M - Horizontal Lined Fill; Z - Triangle

5) **d** - J - Eight shapes; S - White Fill

6) **a** - V - Grey Fill; G - Pentagon points downwards

7) **c** - R - Medium Outline; E - Enclosed Circle has a Black Fill

8) **a** - J - Rounded Square Shape; O - White Fill

9) **b** - D - Triangles; P - Grey Fill

Section B

Example - **a** - Solved horizontally: The figure has been rotated 90° clockwise. The Black Fill has become Grey.

1) **b** - Solved horizontally: The figure has been rotated 180°.

2) **a** - Solved horizontally: The fills have moved one position inwards. The fill of the square has become White.

3) **b** - Solved horizontally or vertically: There must be one Triangle, one Circle and one Square. There must be one White Fill, one Black Fill and one Grey Fill.

4) **c** - Solved horizontally: The figure has been rotated 90° anticlockwise.

5) **a** - Solved horizontally: The large shape has been flipped vertically. The fill of the smaller outer shape has become the fill of the enclosed shape. The original outer shape has been rotated 180° and has swapped positions with the enclosed shape.

6) **e** - Solved horizontally or vertically: There must be one Square, one Circle and one Pentagon. There must be one figure with one Dot, one figure with two Dots and one figure with three Dots.

7) **b** - Solved horizontally: There must be one figure pointing to the top left corner and one figure pointing to the bottom left corner. There must be one vertical figure with a line overlaying the Circle.

8) **d** - Solved vertically: One vertical Line has been added.

Section C

Example - **b** - The figure rotates 90° clockwise. One Arrow is subtracted.

1) **d** - The fill of the enclosed shape becomes the fill of the next outer shape. The Triangle rotates 90° clockwise.

2) **b** - The order of line types of the Circle is: Thin, Thick, Thin, Thin, Thick. The order of line types of the Square is: Thick, Thin, Thin, Thick, Thin. The fill of the Square alternates between Grey and White.

Answers

3) **a** - One of the Black Fills moves one position clockwise.

4) **c** - The figure flips horizontally and swaps position with the Circle(s). The number of Circles is: 1, 2, 3, 2, 1.

5) **e** - Two Circles are removed and two Squares are added. The figure flips horizontally.

6) **b** - The number of Lines around the enclosed figure is: 2, 3, 4, 0, 1. The number of Lines attached to the Circle is: 3, 2, 1, 0, 4.

7) **a** - The figure rotates 90° clockwise. The order of fills is: Vertical Lined, Horizontal Lined, Diagonal Lined, Vertical Lined, Horizontal Lined.

8) **b** - The number of Stars alternates between two and one. Two Circles are subtracted. One Square is added.

9) **b** - The figure flips horizontally. One Arrow is subtracted from the top and bottom alternately.

10) **d** - The Arrows move one position to the right. The Circle moves one position to the left. The fill of the Circle alternates between White and Black.

Section D

Example - **d** - The figure is not Straight-edged.

1) **b** - The overlaying shapes are not the same as the large shape.

2) **c** - The figure is not divided into six sections.

3) **b** - The total number of Dots in the figure is not an odd number.

4) **b** - The number of Lines enclosed in the Circle does not equal the number of sides of the outer shapes.

5) **c** - There is not one more Square than Circle.

6) **d** - The figure is an inversion, not a rotation of the others.

7) **a** - The enclosed shapes are not the same.

8) **c** - The order of outlines is not Thick, Thin, Thick.

Non-verbal Reasoning Test 4
Section A

Example - **d** - The figure rotates 90° clockwise. The fill becomes White.

1) **b** - The figure rotates 180°. The Lined Fill rotates 90°. The fill of the enclosed shape becomes Black.

2) **c** - A larger replica of the figure is added, enclosing the original. The original figure rotates 180° and the fill becomes Black.

3) **a** - The figure rotates 90° clockwise. The White Fill becomes Grey.

4) **a** - The fills move one position anticlockwise. The figure rotates 180°.

5) **d** - The figure enclosed in the middle right square moves two positions anticlockwise. The other enclosed figures move three positions anticlockwise. The outline becomes Thick.

6) **a** - The figure rotates 90° clockwise. The order of fills, in a clockwise direction, becomes: Grey, Black, Grey, White.

7) **c** - The figure rotates 90° clockwise and enlarges.

8) **e** - The figure rotates 180°. The Solid Horizontal Line becomes a Dotted Vertical Line.

9) **a** - The two inner shapes swap positions. The new central shape becomes squashed. The new middle shape becomes stretched. The outer shape becomes an Ellipse.

Section B

Example - **a** - Solved horizontally: The figure has been rotated 90° clockwise. The Black Fill has become Grey.

1) **c** - Solved vertically: The figure has been reflected vertically along the horizontal mid-line of the matrix. The fills have been swapped.

2) **d** - Solved horizontally: The figure has been rotated 90° clockwise and one Square has been subtracted.

Answers

3) **e** - Solved horizontally: There must be one Pentagon, one Square and one Triangle. The figures in columns 1 and 3 must be the same fill.

4) **c** - Solved horizontally: The figure has been rotated 90° clockwise. The Lines have been spaced out evenly. A reflection of the shapes has been added to fill the square.

5) **c** - Solved horizontally: The figure has been reflected along the vertical mid-line of the matrix.

6) **a** - Solved horizontally: The figure with two Lines has been rotated 90° and added to the figure with one Line to create the figure with three Lines.

7) **d** - Solved horizontally: The figure has been rotated 90°. There must be two fills that are the same and one fill that must be different.

8) **b** - Solved horizontally: There must be the same number of shapes in each square.

Section C

Example - **c** - A - Circle; Y - Grey Fill

1) **b** - G - Small figure; L - Horizontal Line enclosed

2) **e** - V - Four sections; W - Black Fill

3) **d** - C - Triangle; R - Dashed Line; H - One Black Fill and one White Fill

4) **a** - Q - Pentagon points downwards; B - Small figure; Y - Circle enclosed

5) **a** - Y - Octagon; N - Black Fill; B - Triangle enclosed

6) **e** - B - Pentagon; P - Horizontal figure; E - Black Fill

7) **c** - G - Vertical figure; T - Grey Fill; X - One Arrowhead

8) **b** - Y - Both Heart Shapes point in the same direction; R - Black Fill

Section D

Example - **a** - The shape has four sides.

1) **e** - Two of the smaller Squares are overlays and two are linkages.

2) **c** - The figure has a Triangle and an Ellipse. Two shapes overlay the third.

3) **c** - There are two identical large Cigar Shapes and two identical small Cigar Shapes. The two large shapes merge. The two small shapes link with the large shapes.

4) **b** - The figure has six sections.

5) **c** - The number of enclosed Circles is equal to one less than the number of sides of the outer shape.

6) **a** - Two smaller replicas of the outer shape are enclosed on one side of the Line, and one different shape is enclosed on the other side of the Line.

7) **c** - Three smaller replicas of the outer shape with Black Fills are overlaid on the edges of the outer shape.

8) **e** - The figure is composed of a Pentagon, an Ellipse and a Rectangle.

9) **e** - The number of enclosed Circles in the figure is equal to the number of sides of the outer shape. One more shape is enclosed.

10) **c** - The figure has two enclosed shapes connected by a Thin Solid Line. The enclosed shape with a White Fill is a smaller replica of the outer shape.

Non-verbal Reasoning Test 5
Section A

Example - **b** - The figure rotates 90° clockwise. One Arrow is subtracted.

1) **c** - The order of fills of the Arrows is: Grey, White, Black, Grey, White. The fill of the Circle alternates between Black and White. The Circle moves one position clockwise.

2) **e** - The number of segments is: 4, 3, 2, 1, 4. The shape alternates between Rectangle and Isosceles Trapezium.

3) **e** - One side is removed from the outer Square and moved to the inner Square.

4) **a** - The figure rotates 90° clockwise. The fills move one position inwards.

5) **b** - The figure rotates 90° clockwise.

6) **a** - The columns of Circles move one position to the right. The fills move one position clockwise.

Answers

7) **e** - The figure rotates 90° clockwise. The fills of the Circles move one position clockwise.

8) **b** - The fill of the Square alternates between Grey and White. The outlines of the Circles increase then decrease in thickness.

9) **c** - The number of Lines and Circles is: 3, 4, 1, 2, 3. The fill of the Circles alternates between Black and White.

Section B

Example - **d** - The figure rotates 90° clockwise. The fill becomes White.

1) **c** - The figure flips horizontally. The figure at the top moves left one position, and flips vertically to be enclosed in the shape.

2) **e** - The figure rotates 180°. The letter on the short vertical Line moves to the long vertical Line.

3) **b** - The original outer shape duplicates, and one encloses the other. The original enclosed shape becomes the outer shape, enclosing the new figure.

4) **a** - The central shape enlarges to enclose the two Circles. The Circles swap position. The outline changes from Solid to Dashed.

5) **c** - The left figure flips vertically, and vertically transposes to underneath the right figure. The White Fill becomes Black.

6) **c** - The large shape is duplicated and placed as a perpendicular merger to the original. One enclosed shape horizontally transposes to the left, into the new shape. The fill of the enclosed shape in the merged section becomes Black.

7) **b** - The figure rotates 180°. One vertical Line is subtracted. The remaining Line(s) become evenly spaced. The enclosed shape then vertically flips.

8) **b** - The figure rotates 90° clockwise. The Black Fill moves two spaces anticlockwise. A Horizontal Line is added to the middle of the Rectangle.

Section C

Example - **d** - The figure is not Straight-edged.

1) **c** - The Arrow does not point away from the Circle.

2) **d** - The Triangles do not all point anticlockwise.

3) **c** - The figure is not a rotation of the other figures.

4) **b** - The outer Triangle is not a rotation of the others.

5) **e** - The figure is not composed of four shapes, creating a four-sided shape in the middle.

6) **e** - The figure does not have seven items on the central Line.

7) **a** - The figure is not a rotation of the other figures.

8) **d** - The smaller Circle does not have a Grey Fill.

Section D

Example - **d** - O - Arrow points upwards;
W - Horizontal Lined Fill

1) **b** - E - Thin Outline; V - Horizontal Lined Fill

2) **d** - E - Enclosure has a White Fill;
J - Triangle enclosed

3) **a** - D - White Fill; Z - Thick Outline

4) **b** - V - Black Fill; F - Rectangles

5) **d** - A - Pentagon enclosed; R - White Fill

6) **a** - N - Three Circles; R - White Fill

7) **e** - R - Triangles; E - Diagonal figure

8) **a** - B - Square has a Black Fill; L - Circle has a Black Fill

9) **c** - H - Thick Outline; R - Horizontal Lined Fill

10) **d** - E - Triangle enclosed; L - Black Fill

Non-verbal Reasoning Test 6
Section A

Example - **a** - The shape has four sides.

1) **d** - The shape has a horizontal line of symmetry.

2) **a** - The figure contains four enclosures. Two of the enclosures are smaller replicas of the outer shape. One of the other two enclosures has a Grey or Black Fill.

Answers

3) **c** - A Circle with a Grey Fill overlays a Circle with a Black Fill. There is a Square with a 45° rotation and a White Fill overlaying both Circles.

4) **e** - The figure is composed of three Triangles, three Rectangles and one Circle.

5) **b** - The Triangle with a White Fill is in the smaller section of the Rectangle. The Line overlays the Triangle with a White Fill.

6) **c** - Two of the three Cigar Shapes overlay one other. The Circle fills alternate between Black and White.

7) **c** - The figure is split into four sections. One Line passes through the shape, and one Line starts and ends outside of the shape. The two Lines intersect. Only one of the Lines goes from a corner.

8) **a** - The order of fills from the top is: White, Grey, Black.

9) **d** - The figure has two of each fill.

Section B

Example - **a** - Solved horizontally: The figure has been rotated 90° clockwise. The Black Fill has become Grey.

1) **a** - Solved vertically: The shapes have swapped positions and fills. The Vertical Lined Fill has become a Horizontal Lined Fill.

2) **d** - Solved horizontally: The figure has been flipped vertically. The Triangle Line Endings have become Circles. The Black and White Fills have been swapped.

3) **b** - Solved horizontally: There must be one small, one medium and one large shape.

4) **b** - Solved vertically: The Line has been reflected horizontally. The middle shape has been stretched and vertically transposed to become the top shape. The top shape has been squashed and vertically transposed to become the middle shape.

5) **e** - Solved vertically: The figure has been rotated 90°. The fills have been swapped.

6) **c** - Solved horizontally and vertically: The figure has been rotated 90° anticlockwise. There must be 1, 2 and 3 Circles with a Cross on each row.

7) **a** - Solved horizontally: The shapes have moved one position upwards. The fills have moved one position downwards.

8) **d** - Solved horizontally: The figure has been rotated 90°. There must be one figure with enclosed Circles, one figure with enclosed Crosses, and one figure with enclosed Squares.

Section C

Example - **b** - The figure rotates 90° clockwise. One Arrow is subtracted.

1) **e** - The figure rotates 135° anticlockwise.

2) **a** - The number of Lines is: 1, 4, 3, 2, 1. The number of Circles is: 3, 4, 1, 2, 3. The Black & White Fills alternate.

3) **c** - One Circle is subtracted. One Cross or Triangle is added alternately.

4) **b** - The fill of the Hexagon alternates between White and Grey. The line types move in by one position.

5) **b** - One small Line is subtracted from the enclosed figure. The number of Lines enclosing the figure is: 2, 3, 4, 0, 1.

6) **a** - The Black and White Fills swap. One Circle is subtracted anticlockwise.

7) **c** - The figure rotates 90° clockwise. One Arrow flips in the order: Grey, Black, White, Grey, Black.

8) **b** - The figure rotates 90° clockwise.

9) **d** - The Circle alternates between being the outer and the enclosed shape. The number of sides of the other shape in the figure is: 4, 5, 3, 4, 5.

10) **b** - The number of Arrows is: 3, 4, 1, 2, 3. The number of Circles is: 3, 4, 1, 2, 3. The fill of the Circles alternates between White and Black. The Arrows horizontally flip.

Answers

Section D

Example - **c** - A - Circle; Y - Grey Fill

1) **c** - X - Square; U - Black Fill
2) **b** - A - Black Fill; H - Triangles point upwards; W - Vertical figure
3) **c** - C - Figure points to the right; M - Black Fill; S - Large figure
4) **c** - C - Hexagon; Y - Enclosed Square; S - White Fill
5) **b** - P - Long Line; V - Square
6) **b** - X - White Fill; G - Outer shape is a Triangle; T - Square enclosed
7) **d** - P - Vertical Line; E - Horizontal Lined Fill; K - Square
8) **e** - B - Triangle points downwards; W - Horizontal figure; J - White Fill

Non-verbal Reasoning Test 7
Section A

Example - **d** - O - Arrow points upwards; W - Horizontal Lined Fill

1) **d** - J - Pentagon; N - Black Fill
2) **b** - M - White Fill; P - Triangle
3) **e** - D - White Fill; Z - Extra Thick Outline
4) **c** - J - Black Fill; W - One Square, one Circle
5) **d** - C - Figure is at the bottom of the square; M - White Fill
6) **d** - R - Figure is in the middle of the square; L - Medium-sized figure
7) **a** - B - White Fill; X - Outer shape is a Circle
8) **d** - D - Arrow points to the left; V - Black Fill
9) **a** - D - Square; T - Triangle points downwards

Section B

Example - **d** - The figure rotates 90° clockwise. The fill becomes White.

1) **a** - The shape with a Black Fill becomes the outer shape. The other two shapes become enclosures. The shape on the right becomes the top enclosed shape with a Black Fill.

2) **c** - The diagonal Lines and the Circle move 180° around the square. The Line connected to the Circle moves 90° clockwise around the square.
3) **d** - The figure rotates 45°. The fills move one position inwards.
4) **d** - The top shape becomes the new outer shape. The original outer shape becomes the top enclosed shape. The two bottom shapes swap positions.
5) **b** - The outer shape rotates 45°. The line types of the Squares swap. The fill of the Circle becomes White.
6) **c** - The figure reflects horizontally. The two small shapes swap fills. The small shape beneath the figure rotates 90° clockwise.
7) **c** - The figure rotates 180°. The White Fill becomes Black. The Lined Fill rotates 90°.
8) **e** - The right side of the figure rotates 180°. The remaining shape horizontally flips and joins to the left side of the first shape.

Section C

Example - **a** - Solved horizontally: The figure has been rotated 90° clockwise. The Black Fill has become Grey.

1) **b** - Solved vertically: The figure has been reflected along the horizontal mid-line of the matrix. The fills have been swapped.
2) **a** - Solved horizontally: The figure has been rotated 45° clockwise. The small shapes have swapped positions and fills. The Rectangles have merged to make a Cross.
3) **b** - Solved horizontally: The Arrow has been rotated 90° clockwise.
4) **c** - Solved vertically: The figure has been rotated 180°.
5) **b** - Solved horizontally: The central figure has been rotated 90° clockwise. The White Fill has become Grey. The Black Fill has become White. The bottom Line has been rotated 90° anticlockwise.

Answers

6) **d** - Solved horizontally: There must be one small, one medium and one large figure.

7) **e** - Solved horizontally: There must be one figure pointing left, one figure pointing right and one figure pointing downwards. There must be one figure with a Black Fill, one figure with a White Fill and one figure with a Vertical Lined Fill.

8) **d** - The matrix is symmetrical.

Section D

Example - **a** - The shape has four sides.

1) **c** - The shape has five sides.

2) **d** - The outer shape has a Thick Outline. The enclosed shape has a Thin Outline.

3) **e** - The figure is a rotation of the Test Figures.

4) **a** - The number of shapes is equal to the number of sides of the shape.

5) **c** - There is one Rectangle, one Circle and one Triangle enclosed in the shape.

6) **c** - Half of the figure has a Black or Grey Fill. The enclosed shape is in the half of the figure with a White Fill and has a different Block Fill.

7) **d** - The order of outlines is: Medium, Thick, Thin, Medium.

8) **b** - There are three shapes overlaying the Circle - one Square, one Circle and one Triangle.

9) **e** - There are four Circles with a Black Fill and four Circles with a White Fill.

10) **a** - The number of smaller shapes is equal to the number of sides of the larger shape.

Non-verbal Reasoning Test 8
Section A

Example - **a** - The shape has four sides.

1) **b** - The middle shape overlays one shape, and another shape overlays the middle shape. The shapes are all different.

2) **d** - The shapes are either all Curved or all Straight-edged. There is one shape with a Black Fill.

3) **b** - There are three Lines and one Circle enclosed in the Shield Shape.

4) **e** - The number of Lines enclosed in the figure is equal to one less than the number of sides of the outer shape.

5) **e** - The Dotted Line is a line of symmetry.

6) **a** - The number of shapes enclosed in the figure is equal to the number of sides of the outer shape. Two of the enclosed shapes have a Grey Fill. The outline of the outer shape is Solid or Dashed.

7) **c** - The order of fills from the back is: Grey, White, Black. The shape with a White Fill overlays the shape with a Grey Fill. The shape with a Black Fill overlays the shape with a White Fill.

8) **c** - There are six Circle Line Endings.

9) **a** - The number of sides totals twelve.

Section B

Example - **b** - The figure rotates 90° clockwise. One Arrow is subtracted.

1) **a** - The figure rotates 90° clockwise. The order of Lined Fills is: Vertical, Horizontal, Diagonal, Vertical, Horizontal.

2) **e** - The Black and White Fills alternate. The order of fills of the central Circle is: White, Grey, Black, White, Grey. The number of short Lines is: 4, 1, 2, 3, 4.

3) **b** - The figure alternates between horizontal and vertical orientation. The order of fills is: White, Black, Grey, White, Black.

4) **b** - The figure rotates 180°. One Line is subtracted. One Circle is added.

5) **d** - The outer shape alternates between Ellipse and Hexagon. The enclosed Circles move one space clockwise alternately.

6) **e** - The number of enclosed Lines alternates between three and four. The number of Circles is reduced by 1. The Black and White Fills swap.

Answers

7) **b** - The order of outer shapes is: Circle, Thick Ellipse, Thin Ellipse, Circle, Thick Ellipse. The Triangle rotates 90° clockwise. The order of fills is: Grey, Black, White, Grey, Black.

8) **a** - The Rectangles move one position to the right.

9) **b** - The horizontal fills swap, then the figure rotates 90° clockwise alternately.

10) **d** - The Pentagon flips vertically. The Circle moves clockwise by one point.

Section C

Example - **d** - The figure is not Straight-edged.

1) **d** - The shape with the Thin Outline is not overlaying the shape with the Thick Outline.

2) **e** - The outer shape is not a rotation of the others.

3) **c** - The Grey Fill sections do not reflect.

4) **d** - The number of shapes is not equal to the number of sides of each shape.

5) **c** - The figure is not symmetrical.

6) **a** - The figure is not a rotation of the others.

7) **d** - The Cross is not enclosed by only one shape.

8) **d** - The figure does not contain a Circle.

Section D

Example - **c** - A - Circle; Y - Grey Fill

1) **d** - E - Figure points to the right; R - Grey Fill; N - Small figure

2) **d** - P - Pentagon points upwards; F - Enclosed Circle with a White Fill

3) **c** - T - Cigar Shape; E - Triangles enclosed; N - White Fill

4) **c** - E - Ellipse; M - Zigzag Line orientation

5) **d** - E - Three Circles have a Black Fill; O - Triangle enclosed

6) **b** - B - Medium Outline; J - Arrow points upwards; X - White Fill

7) **c** - B - Vertical figure; T - Cross; G - One Grey Fill and one Black Fill

8) **b** - S - Star has a White Fill; X - Star points downwards; B - Square has a Grey Fill

Notes

Notes

PROGRESS CHARTS

Test 1

Section A	(9)	_____
Section B	(8)	_____
Section C	(8)	_____
Section D	(10)	_____
Total Score	_____	
Percentage	_____%	

Test 2

Section A	(8)	_____
Section B	(9)	_____
Section C	(8)	_____
Section D	(10)	_____
Total Score	_____	
Percentage	_____%	

Test 3

Section A	(9)	_____
Section B	(8)	_____
Section C	(10)	_____
Section D	(8)	_____
Total Score	_____	
Percentage	_____%	

Test 4

Section A	(9)	_____
Section B	(8)	_____
Section C	(8)	_____
Section D	(10)	_____
Total Score	_____	
Percentage	_____%	

Test 5

Section A	(9)	_____
Section B	(8)	_____
Section C	(8)	_____
Section D	(10)	_____
Total Score	_____	
Percentage	_____%	

Test 6

Section A	(9)	_____
Section B	(8)	_____
Section C	(10)	_____
Section D	(8)	_____
Total Score	_____	
Percentage	_____%	

Test 7

Section A	(9)	_____
Section B	(8)	_____
Section C	(8)	_____
Section D	(10)	_____
Total Score	_____	
Percentage	_____%	

Test 8

Section A	(9)	_____
Section B	(10)	_____
Section C	(8)	_____
Section D	(8)	_____
Total Score	_____	
Percentage	_____%	

Overall Percentage | **%** | For the average add up % and divide by 8

CERTIFICATE OF

ACHIEVEMENT

This certifies

_____

has successfully completed

11+ Non-verbal Reasoning
Year 5–7
TESTBOOK **2**

Overall percentage
score achieved

[ ] **%**

Comment _____

_____

Signed _____

(teacher/parent/guardian)

Date _____